TZEDAKAH

The *Basic Jewish Ideas* Series

Series Editor: Jacob Neusner

TZEDAKAH

*Can Jewish
Philanthropy Buy
Jewish Survival?*

Jacob Neusner

 Chappaqua, NY

Published by Rossel Books, 44 Dunbow Drive,
Chappaqua, New York 10514 (914) 238-8954

Library of Congress Cataloging in Publication Data

Neusner, Jacob, 1932–
  Tzedakah.

  (The Basic Jewish ideas series)
  Bibliography: p.
  1. Charity laws and legislation (Jewish law)
2. Jews—Charities. I. Title. II. Series.
LAW   296.3'85   82-18552
ISBN 0-940646-02-1

First Edition

Cover art by Mordechai Rosenstein
© 1982 by Emes Editions, Ltd.

Book and cover design by Carol Isaak

Chapter illustrations by Leslie Cober

ACKNOWLEDGMENTS

Seymour Rossel gave me the idea for this book. Professor David Altshuler, George Washington University, served as my editor, supplying much good criticism. David Weiner prepared the Hebrew texts, and their literal translations, which form the appendix.

For
Carmi Schwartz
and
Darrell Friedman

CONTENTS

TZEDAKAH

Torah and Tzedakah

This book speaks to Jews who spend their lives working for Jewish organizations and institutions—to Jews who give of their own time, energy, intelligence, and leadership to raise funds and to decide how and when community monies shall be disbursed.

By definition, the work of the organizations and institutions of the Jewish community is a labor of *tzedakah* (the Hebrew word that means both "righteousness" and "charity"). Tzedakah involves support of Jewish education and day schools, hospitals, homes for the aged, programs in the State of Israel and overseas, work for the protection of Jewish rights everywhere and for saving Jews in trouble. All these constitute the labors of tzedakah. The issue central to this book is how to place the tzedakah people do into the framework of Judaism, that is to say, of Torah—or to put it differently, how to make sense of acts of tzedakah in the setting of the inner life of Torah.

It is an urgent problem. The work of tzedakah in the Jewish community absorbs much of the energy of devoted Jews. A theory is therefore necessary to make sense of practice; a context is needed for doing what we already believe we should do. This book sets forth the thesis that revealing the full and rich meaning of tzedakah in the setting of Torah, of Judaism, will make it possible for those who do tzedakah to become still more devoted and enlightened Jewishly. Understanding what we do makes the deed still more important than it already is.

Tzedakah for many is a way of being Jewish, a Jewish way of life. That is as it should be. The task ahead is to investigate what that Jewish way of life means—the beliefs expressed through behavior. For, to a great extent, we are what we do.

Secular and Religious

Many people think that in the setting of the Jewish community it is possible to distinguish secular from religious. Raising money is said to be secular. Praying or studying Jewish holy books ("Torah") is religious. According to that view, raising money does not make one a "better Jew" (let alone a "good Jew"), while, for example, participating in a Passover Seder does. The sources of Judaism assembled in this book— specifically, classical statements of both Jewish law and Jewish theology—prove that distinction is wrong. *Tzedakah is the highest expression of the holy way of living taught by Torah.*

Now that allegation may sound self-evident to people who do most of what they do as Jews in the framework of organizations and institutions, performing *mitzvot* ("religious deeds") through raising funds for tzedakah. Yet it bears within itself complications and demands. The demands will be seen in the study of the texts. The complications are right before us.

People involved in Jewish community work face a subtle irony. They spend their lives in Jewish organizations. Yet what they do seems on the surface to be neutral, not particularly Jewish. What people active in Jewish life ask themselves is the reason behind what they are doing. The committee meetings, the paper work, the drudgery—they give so much in such humble ways. Is the end merely the honor of an office, one's picture in the local Jewish paper, a name on a plaque? All of us need some ego-food. But only a minority, unusually devoted people, do the work of the Jewish organizations and communal institutions.

Are we to be satisfied merely because we have done good? If that is our final word on the matter, we end up taking a narrow this-worldly view of this gift of ours, I mean, the gift of our life. Surely there is more to the labor of communty service than self-satisfaction, either of the gross variety, or of the more spiritual kind. And the "more" that there must be derives from Judaism.

My purpose in this book is to study some of the important teachings of Judaism. I promise two things: First, we shall learn things useful today from the wisdom of the Jewish sages, expressed both in laws and in moral teachings, about work they then did and we now do. Second, at the end I shall raise some deeper questions about the other mitzvot, beyond the *mitzvah* of tzedakah, awaiting our attention.

In this manner, I hope to speak to people who do the great deeds of drudgery, and therefore need some explanation of the context and meaning of the great deeds they do. If in the end I help some member of Hadassah, for example, to do the detailed work of that important organization by showing her how in today's world she obeys and embodies the law of Judaism, I shall have made that modest contribution I should like to make to the ongoing life of Israel, the Jewish people.

So we begin by asking for the Torah of tzedakah: What are we supposed to do? What does what we are supposed to do mean about what we are supposed to be? These are the two questions to keep in mind.

What Is Torah?

When we want to know what Judaism says, we turn to Torah. Now *Torah* (literally, "revelation") bears a range of meanings, expanding from age to age. In this sense, Torah is open-ended and includes you and me. The principal source of revelation is, of course, *the* Torah, the Five Books of Moses. The *Neviim*, the books of the Prophets; and the *Ketuvim*, the sacred Writings (such as Psalms, Proverbs, the Five Scrolls, and the like); together with the Torah, constitute *TaNaKh*, the canonical Hebrew Scriptures. This collection, which Christians call the "Old Testament," is called "written Torah" by our ancient rabbis.

These same rabbis refer to the literature that emanated from their own movement as "oral Torah." The oral Torah includes the *Mishnah*, produced about 200 C.E., and two *Talmuds*—one for the Land of Israel and another for Babylonia— each built upon the Mishnah in the next several centuries. Oral Torah also includes many compilations of *midrash*, rabbinic exegesis of the *Tanakh*.

Taken together, then, biblical "written Torah" and rabbinic "oral Torah" form what the sages of Judaism call "the whole Torah," one integral living body of revelation they attribute to Moses "our rabbi" (*Moshe Rabbenu*). From that time forward, as the great Jewish minds continue to explore and explain, each generation's work is also received as Torah.

For Judaism, as for any historic religious tradition, you cannot make things up as you go along, or say what sounds right or feels good, calling it "Judaism." True, you are right for yourself in whatever you say. But to speak to someone else in the framework of Judaism, you must speak a common language. the conversation is three-sided: you, the other person, and the great body of law and theology called Torah.

A Foretaste of Torah

Before turning to the law, which is concrete and specific, let us begin with a passage of theology, which is general and immediate. The passage cited below tells the story of a king who ruled part of Mesopotamia (present-day Iraq) in the first century of the common era. He is supposed to have converted to Judaism, and tales of things he did fill the pages of talmudic literature as models of righteousness and justice.

This particular story is important for two reasons. It shows us the fundamental value placed upon tzedakah by the rabbis who repeated the tale and by the Jews who from then to now shaped their lives, in part, around the value expressed in it. And it shows how when we read each biblical verse on "righteousness" as a statement on "charity"—as the word tzedakah = righteousness & charity requires us to do—we find quite striking teachings about tzedakah.

This passage appears in the *Tosefta*, which means "Supplement." The Tosefta supplements the Mishnah. Once the Mishnah came to closure (about 200 C.E., as previously stated), further materials were collected to augment and amplify what the Mishnah contained. Over the next two hundred years or so, the Tosefta took shape, side by side with the two Talmuds. This imaginary conversation is the Tosefta's complement to a passage of the Mishnah on gifts to the poor.

> **Monobases, King of Adiabene, dispensed his treasures during the years of famine. When his brothers heard, they sent him the following message, "Your ancestors stored up treasures and increased the wealth they inherited. But you went and gave to the poor all of the royal treasures, both your own and those of your ancestors."**
>
> **Monobases replied, "My ancestors stored up treasures for this world below, but I have stored up**

treasures for the world above, as it is stated, *Faithful-ness will spring up from the ground below, and right-eousness will look down from the sky.* My ancestors stored up treasures where the hand [of thieves] can reach, but I have stored up treasures where no [thieves'] hand can reach, as it is stated, *Righteousness and jus-tice are the foundation of Your throne, steadfast love and faithfulness go before You.* My ancestors stored up treasures that produce no [real] benefits, but I have stored up treasures that produce benefits, as it is stated, *Tell the righteous that it shall be well with them, for they shall reap the benefits of their deeds.* My ancestors stored up treasures of money, but I have stored up trea-sures of souls, as it is stated, *The fruit of the righteous is a tree of life, and a wise person saves the souls of the poor.* My ancestors stored up treasures that [after their deaths] would benefit only others, but I have stored up treasures that will benefit myself [both in my lifetime and after my death], as it is stated, *It shall be accounted righteousness to you before the Lord your God.* My ancestors stored up treasures for this world, but I have stored up treasures for myself in the world-to-come, as it is stated, *Your righteousness shall go before you, and the glory of the Lord shall be your rear guard.*"*

The meaning is clearly that tzedakah is for all time. What we do for tzedakah lasts. People cannot touch the treasure of tze-dakah. Material wealth is for this world. Tzedakah is for the soul. Material wealth ends with the grave. Tzedakah is for eter-nity. Material wealth is for amassing. Tzedakah benefits my world. How secular, we must ask ourselves, is our work in tzedakah? As the story evaluates it, the supposedly "secular" deed of writing a check, making a phone call, sitting in a meet-ing, working on a budget—all these must in fact be holy.

---

*Translations of classical sources cited in this work are given in paraphrases of the original. Hebrew or Aramaic originals, vocalized and accompanied by more literal translations, may be found in the *Appendix*, beginning on page 81.

The story of Monobases is a theological statement on the meaning of tzedakah. It states the Torah's basic evaluation of tzedakah in general terms. But, we are what we do. The answer of Monobases is as pertinent today as it was when it was recorded; and the questions it raises as relevant to us as they were relevant then.

Throughout the discussions of the laws that appear in the next several chapters, we shall continually ask these questions. What kinds of deeds of tzedakah are we supposed to do? And how do these deeds help to define and express what, as Jews and human beings, we are?

Laws Concerning Degrees of Tzedakah

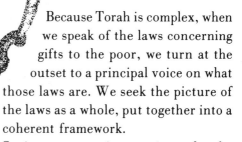

Because Torah is complex, when we speak of the laws concerning gifts to the poor, we turn at the outset to a principal voice on what those laws are. We seek the picture of the laws as a whole, put together into a coherent framework.

Sayings on any given topic tend to be scattered throughout the written and oral Torahs. The Torahs are not organized as topical outlines, but in other ways entirely. Happily, there were medieval scholars who drew the laws together into well-organized codes, set up around principles of general interest. A code of law, like any code today, was meant for ready reference. It summarizes the law and sets it out in readily accessible form. These medieval codes repeat the Torah, and the code we consult is called *Mishneh Torah*, literally, "a repetition of the Torah," that is, a review of the whole.

The authority who compiled this law code is Moses Maimonides (1135–1204 C.E.). The importance of the Mishneh

Torah which he wrote is not that it gives the opinion of a great
rabbi, but actually that it does not. It is public, not personal.
The contents of the book, in general, derive from the Tanakh,
the Talmuds, and related, authoritative legal literature of
Judaism. The reason we turn to the Mishneh Torah, therefore,
is that it provides us with a reliable, accurate, and succinct
picture of the Jewish law of tzedakah.

Maimonides treats tzedakah within the seventh book of his
code, *The Book of Agriculture,* where he summarizes a wide
range of rules governing how people conduct the business of
farming. Since in the time of the Mishnah and the Talmuds, the
Jews mostly were engaged in agriculture, these laws address the
core of economic life as it was then structured. It is appropriate
to consider giving away money or goods in the very setting
where wealth is formed. Resources allow people the opportunity
to engage in tzedakah. Accordingly, Maimonides' choice for the
larger setting in which to discuss tzedakah is sensible and
reasonable.

Maimonides does two things in this treatise on tzedakah: He
provides a picture of the whole—the laws seen from afar, the
main point of it all. He also presents many individual rules. We
begin with the overview; then, in the following two chapters, we
take up some of the specific rules.

The Eight Stages of Tzedakah

> There are eight degrees of tzedakah, each one superior
> to the next. The highest degree, than which there is
> none higher, is the one who upholds the hand of an
> Israelite reduced to poverty by handing that person a
> gift or loan, or by entering into a partnership with him
> or her, or by finding that Israelite work, in order to
> strengthen that person's hand, so that she or he will
> have no need to beg from others. Concerning such a
> person it is stated, *You shall uphold that one, as a
> stranger and a settler shall that person live with you*—
> meaning, uphold that person, so that she or he will not
> lapse into want.

Below this is one who gives alms to the poor in such a way that the giver knows not to whom the alms are given, nor does the poor person know from whom the alms are received. This constitutes the fulfilling of a religious duty for its own sake, and for such there was a Chamber of Secrets in the Temple, where the righteous would contribute sums secretly, and where the poor of good families would draw their sustenance in equal secrecy. Close to such a person is the one who contributes directly to the charity fund. (One should not, however, give directly to the charity fund unless it has been ascertained that the person in charge of it is trustworthy, a sage, who knows how to administer it properly, as was the case [when it was directed by the hand] of Rabbi Hananiah ben Teradyon.)

Below this is the person who knows the one receiving while the poor person knows not from whom the gift comes. Such a donor is like the great among the sages who would set forth secretly, throwing money before the doors of the poor. This is an appropriate procedure, to be preferred if those administering charity funds are not behaving honorably.

Below this is the instance in which the poor knows the identity of the donor, but remains unknown to the donor. The giver is thus like the great among the sages who would place money in the folded corner of a linen sheet, throw the sheet over their shoulders, and allow the poor to come up behind them and remove the money without being subject to humiliation.

Below this is the one who hands charity directly to the poor before being asked for it.

Below this is the one who hands charity to the poor after the poor has requested it.

Below this is the one who gives to the poor less than what is appropriate, but gives it in a friendly manner.

Below this is the one who gives charity with a scowl.

The great among the sages used to hand a small coin to a poor person before praying and then to pray, as it is stated, *As for me, I shall behold Your face in righteousness.*

The Main Points

The laws before us present three principles:

1. The way to deal with poverty is to help the poor help themselves.

2. When one gives tzedakah to the poor, the way to do it is so that the left hand does not know what the right hand is doing, so to speak. The poor are respected; the donors remain anonymous.

This second point is spelled out in the following stages:

A. The poor do not know who has given; the donors do not know to whom the money goes.

B. The donors know; the poor do not.

C. The poor know; the donors do not.

3. The final principle is essentially a repetition of the main point of the second: the dignity of the poor must be respected. This is spelled out in four further stages:

A. The donors give (what is required) without being asked.

B. The donors give (what is required) only when asked.

C. The donors give less than is proper, but in a friendly way.

D. The donors give in an unfriendly way.

In all, the Jewish law before us makes one fundamental point, namely, the poor person must enjoy self-respect and dignity.

The best way to give is not to give, but to lend, thus helping the poor person make his or her own livelihood. That stands outside of the framework of "charity," but it is central to the realm of tzedakah. The second group of laws seeks to preserve the anonymity of the act of tzedakah, since this allows the poor person's dignity to be preserved. The third then restates the same matter in a more personal way: not being asked, being asked, giving in a friendly way, in an unfriendly way.

"In the Image of God"

What the law requires, therefore, is consideration for the humanity of the poor person, who remains no different from us who give. The poor are not less than us or different from us. They have not only needs, but also feelings. They want not only bread, but also respect.

When we give to the poor, we must do so in such a way that the equality of the giver and receiver is acknowledged. This is not an act of grace or an expression of affection. It is an act of respect, an expression of duty. The use of the word tzedakah in the sense of doing what is right and required is deliberate and definitive. We give not because we feel like it, but because it is our obligation. We do so in a way that will not make us feel superior, and in a way that will not make the poor person feel inferior.

For this reason we begin with the notion that the best way to do tzedakah is to find work for the poor, to relieve the poor of the necessity of begging. Failing that, the next best thing is to ensure that we do not discover who is receiving our charity, in order that we not develop a sense of self-importance, thinking ourselves "Lady Bountifuls." It is less suitable if the donor knows but the recipient does not know the source of the funds. Still, the recipient enjoys dignity. Finally, the poor person may know the source of the money; the wealthy one not know the recipient.

How to Give

We notice two things: First, it is not appropriate for the donor to know who gets, the recipient to know who gives. We attempt to preserve the dignity of the poor even under less than ideal circumstances.

Second, the situation of the donor is as important as that of the recipient. We care very much about how the donor thinks and feels about the act of tzedakah. It is not enough to give. Giving must be done with thought. It must be marked by reflection, respect for the other party, and hence humility on the part of the donor. How the money is handed over—in the worst case, in which the giver hands it directly to the recipient—is subject to a simple rule: It must be done with regard and in friendship. It must not be done in a mean and niggardly spirit.

Accordingly, the bottom line is this: how you do it matters at least as much as what you do; and, I am inclined to think, even more. That is the meaning of the laws of tzedakah. In a sense, the law has a high opinion of us all. It seeks to ensure dignity and honor for us all, despite a particular need to give or to receive. No, rather say, not despite but through tzedakah!

Donor and recipient are equally in the image and likeness of God. Though the one appears powerful and the other weak, the one who gives (as we shall see later) "greets the Presence of God." The weakness of the poor person stands for God. We are strong so that, in giving, we may become less rich, less powerful; we are in need so that, in receiving, we may give to the giver. We seek power and wealth so as to achieve. The laws, through detail, give form and body to the soul and heart. So we move from what is required of us to what we are required to become.

FOR OUR COMMUNITY

Having studied the source, it is necessary to consider how it is relevant to the work of tzedakah in the Jewish community today—to us. What vision of us as individuals and as a holy people does this text convey?

We need both concrete deeds and a vision. The one without the other is null. If we do deeds of tzedakah without a vision of ourselves, the result must be a sense of drudgery. We do not gain for our own lives the riches contained within our deeds of tzedakah. If, on the other hand, we have a vision of ourselves but no concrete deeds, we are not worthy of the vision.

Yet at each such point in this book, a problem arises which only you, the reader, can solve. This book is directed to those who participate in the United Jewish Appeal and community Federations, the Organization for Rehabilitation and Training (ORT), International B'nai B'rith, Hadassah, and all the other great instruments of tzedakah created and supported by our community. Yet no single volume can encompass the specific work done by so many vast institutions. Clearly, only you know precisely where you are and what you are doing. I may imagine the drudgery, the need for inspiration. But if this book has reached the right hands, then you are the one who sits in the chair, listening to the speeches. You are also the one who gets the enjoyment of the shared labor, who participates in the special sense of community evoked by tzedakah. You have to develop a "code of Jewish law" for the community today, just as Maimonides, deriving his wisdom from the riches of Judaism through the ages, made such a code. You, in essence—through discussion and introspection—must help write this book even as you read it, by filling in that which is particular to you.

But what does the passage on degrees of tzedakah require us to be? (It is clear what is required of us, for that is stated outright by Maimonides.) What kind of person does the passage address?

The law treats us, its readers who are required to follow it, as people who respect themselves and do not wish to achieve superiority through conceiving of others as inferior. People with dignity believe in doing their duty. They gain satisfaction by doing what is required before or without being told what is required. So, at their best, they give anonymously, to an unknown person.

Laws Concerning Distribution of Tzedakah

Having seen a systemic and general statement, we turn to specific laws as formulated by Maimonides out of the resources of Jewish law found in Scripture, the Mishnah and Talmuds, and in related writings accumulated in the two thousand or so years before the codifier's time. We take up six practical rules and examine each of them briefly (and examine six more in the following chapter). In each case, our purpose is the same. We ask what may be learned now from these laws of ancient and medieval times. So we move from general to particular and back to general points.

Clearly, the philosophy of tzedakah centers upon how we *treat* the poor. The ladder of virtues constructed by Maimonides leaves no doubt about this. So to move from ideals to concrete decisions, we examine first of all six laws that deal with how the poor are to be treated: what we owe them, what we do not owe them.

1. What Do the Poor Have to Do
for Themselves?

**The owner of houses, fields, and vineyards, which, if
they are sold during the rainy season would bring a low
price, but if held back to be sold in the summer would
bring a fair price, may not be forced to sell. [The fields,
houses, and vineyards] should be maintained out of the
tithe set aside for the poor up to half their value. A
person should not feel pressed to sell at the wrong time.**

The law refers to a setting in which land is more valuable when
it is growing a crop than when it is lying fallow. The rainy
season is not a time for sowing. Land is consequently worth less.
Cash is expensive at that time, too, since there is outlay but
little income. In the summer, when the field bears crops, it is
worth more. Accordingly, the poor person may not be forced to
sell property at a disadvantageous season or into a saturated
market.

The law implies, without stating, that it is not a sin or a
crime to be poor. Poverty is part of life. If a poor person is in
need but has some assets, we do not demand that the person sell
off those assets without regard to market conditions. That
would be punitive, manifestly unfair. The fact that the poor
have assets is not held against them; and the poor are not
subjected to demands or conditions not applicable to everyone
else.

But there are limits: "up to half their value. . . ." The
community at large may not be burdened without regard to the
prospects of the poor person. There is a compromise to be nego-
tiated between the demands of the poor, which are legitimate
and must be met, and the fair treatment of the assets of the
community as a whole which must be respected. So the poor
must be maintained, without enforced sales or bankruptcies.
But the poor must also utilize their assets at the right time.

FOR OUR COMMUNITY

When a means test is applied by a tzedakah fund or agency,
rules have been set prescribing a balance such as that struck in
the law above. You are supposed to weigh the needs of the needy
against the resources of the community. In this way, we are
required to be people of judgment, able and willing to take the
risk of making a guess.

2. *What Does the Community Have to Do for the Poor?*

**You are commanded to provide for the poor person
according to what the poor person lacks. If it be
clothing, the poor should be clothed. If it be furnish-
ings for the home, they should be purchased for the
poor. If a poor man lacks a wife, he should be helped to
marry. If it be a woman, she should be given in marriage. Even if [the person before becoming poor] was
used to riding a horse and having a servant run before
it, and has now become poor and lacks possessions, a
horse to ride and a servant to run before must be provided, as it is stated, *Sufficient for one's need in that
which one wants.* You are thus commanded to fill the
poor one's want; but you are not obligated to restore the
poor person's wealth.**

The law requires us to take account of the standing and status of
the poor person. First, the poor must be given whatever is
lacking or whatever is needed. Second, the psychological, as
much as the material, needs of the poor must be met. In the
setting of the law, which has in mind a person once but no
longer wealthy, we speak of having a horse and even a herald.
These must be provided. The proof text, drawn from Deuteronomy, then serves to indicate that fact: "Sufficient for one's
need. . . ." The need is relative to the person.

Being poor is not a sentence to death. It is something that can happen to anyone—to you, the law implies—therefore, the necessity to treat the poor person with dignity and respect. If some one of us falls into need, we do not supply only the bare minimum of funds to keep that person alive. We try to preserve the person's condition in life. Once more, however, the law balances one thing against another. You are required to meet the person's needs. You are not required to restore the poor to wealth. The community takes care of the poor. It is not obligated to make the poor rich (hence, too: the rich poor). We recall that the highest form of tzedakah is to help the poor person find a job and become self-sufficient. Here is the corollary to that principle: You help the poor person, you do not have to make the poor person as rich as had once been the case (or had never been the case).

FOR OUR COMMUNITY

There are many sorts of needs for which tzedakah must suffice. What is striking in this rule is not only the notion that the poor must be helped in accord with their dignity. It is also that tzedakah extends to acts of supporting not merely the physical well-being but also the health of the whole person: marriage, luxuries essential to a person's life. Now, in the stern climate of Western civilization, the poor person is housed, fed, and clothed, but the spirit is seldom nourished. Jewish law attends to poverty in a deep sense. That means, of course, that we too may be poor in some ways, just as we are wealthy in others. The detail about providing a horse and herald indicates that matters are relative. We are required to be whole people, not merely bags of money or arbiters of the public welfare. Tzedakah is giving not only of money but also of heart. Thus the law regards us as people with heart to give; people with care and concern for one another.

3. *How Do You Know the Poor Person Really Is Poor?*

If a poor stranger appears and says, "I am hungry; give me something to eat," do not question whether or not the stranger is an imposter—provide food immediately. If, however, the stranger has no clothing and says, "Give me clothing," then question to see if it is a case of possible fraud. If the person is known, provide clothing immediately in the style best suited to the person's dignity, without further inquiry.

The law here distinguishes two kinds of needs: immediate and long-term. An immediate need is a case of hunger. Here we supply what is needed without asking questions. A long-term need is not urgent; therefore, we make certain that the need is real. In talmudic times there were two separate funds for this purpose. One was a kind of soup kitchen, always open for the needy. All the poor had to do was to come and take what was needed. The other was a charity fund, distributed once a week to those on the list of the needy.

You never can be sure that someone who says, "I am hungry," really is hungry. You do not have to be sure. You take people at face value—when it comes to an emergency. If a person is hungry, you give food, and ask questions later. If someone is cold, you provide heating, and then look into the matter. So much for emergencies. But when it comes to things that can be postponed, you do have the obligation to make certain the claim is valid. Obviously, if the poor person is known, you provide clothing without further inquiry. The main point comes at the outset, therefore, and stresses that in matters of tzedakah, you give first and ask questions later.

But you do ask questions. That means that the law is deeply concerned not to waste money set aside for tzedakah. So there has to be a balance between the demands of an emergency and responsibilities over the long term. The donor who wants merely to give and then to walk away cannot do so. The donor must stick around and make certain the money is properly used. You respond to emergency with good will. But emotion is not everything. There must be consideration. Give, then examine.

FOR OUR COMMUNITY

Here, as in the previous two rules, there is a balance to be struck. We already know that we are required to weigh the needs of the poor with those of the community, and that we must measure our efforts to aid the poor according to psychological as well as financial standards. Now we are instructed to balance community responsiveness and concern, on the one hand, with public accountability and caution, on the other. Those who administer allocations of tzedakah funds are responsible for all aspects of an ongoing process of action and study, study and action.

4. *Who Comes First?*

A poor person who is one's relative has priority over all others, the poor within one's household have priority over other poor within one's city, and the poor within one's city have priority over the poor of another city, as it is stated, *To your poor and needy brother, in your land.*

The proof text, again from Deuteronomy, refers to "your . . . needy brother, in your land." This is taken as a warrant to help the poor nearby before turning to the needs of the poor in distant places. Since, in our own setting, "poor" stands for the needs of the Jewish community at large, the message is not difficult to translate.

The law is clear and unequivocal. Help the poor nearby before the poor far away: relative, household, city, and outward from there. The principle is less obvious than it seems. It is easier to feel sympathy for starving people somewhere else than to care for the seemingly lazy louts near at hand. Out there, beyond the town you live in, are people without flaw and in need. But here where you see who needs and why, you may not find the matter pressing. After all, you may well feel superior to your poor relative, or to poor people near at hand. You made it; they didn't. What do you owe them if you started out equal?

So we have a psychological motive to prefer to spread our generosity over hills and across oceans, to treat the poor near at hand as though they were not poor at all, but somehow inadequate. Life is easier when we do not see the nearer problems; if the poor may become invisible, we may go about our business with an easier conscience. For the poor make the rest of us uncomfortable. They bring out conflicting emotions: generosity, but also superiority; concern, but also a sense of power. These other feelings, superiority and power, leave us with a further sense—that of guilt. So it is easier to ignore the whole matter, at the same time giving generously for someone far away. That way seems to resolve all problems. Jewish law prohibits it.

FOR OUR COMMUNITY

The poor in our own town stand for all the beneficiaries of Jewish organizational life, whether the young people in youth groups or old people in programs for the aged, or the schools, or Jewish studies programs in local colleges and universities. The entire range of local services fall within the context of the present law: priority first for the people at home. They have nowhere else to turn. At the same time, in this day and age, what can we honestly consider the limits of our town? A long journey in the time of Maimonides would correspond to an easy commute in our own day. In fact we live in a global village.

The criterion now must be, what priorities should govern allocations for a long future? That is to say, without regard to geography, but considering only the future of this community as part of the whole Jewish people, what comes first? It may be that a youth program bringing young Americans for work and study in the State of Israel, involving the best of the youth of your own town, is more vital for all Israel, the Jewish people, and at the same time more effective for your community, than an alternative program of greater local visibility. These are issues requiring the exercise of judgment and even taste. We are required to be people of international vision at this moment in history. We cannot allow ourselves to become parochial or isolationist.

5. *Helping Gentiles Too*

> One is required to feed and clothe the non-Jewish poor together with the poor of Israel, this for the sake of the ways of peace. In the case of a poor person going from door to door, one is not required to give such a person a large gift, but only a small one. It is forbidden, however, to allow a poor person who asks for charity to go away empty-handed—you must give at least a dry fig, as it is stated, *Let not the oppressed turn away in confusion.*

This law is the complement to the one that preceded it. Just as we help the poor near at hand before helping the alien poor, so we help the non-Jews in need as well as the Jews. The law takes for granted a world in which there is much begging. Those who have visited the State of Israel or other Middle Eastern, African, and Asian countries probably have a fairly hostile view of personal begging, which is embarrassing and annoying. In the setting in which Maimonides formulated the law, and for a thousand and more years before that time, begging was commonplace. Indeed, in the setting of Judaism, in which giving was and is tzedakah, begging gave the donor a chance to acquire the merit of giving, hence, to fulfill the mitzvah of tzedakah. Accordingly, in the Talmud of the Land of Israel there are many stories in which a beggar says to a donor, "Acquire merit through me," meaning, "Give me tzedakah." The beggar bestows something, just as the donor does. In the present law, the simple point is that, whoever comes to your door, give something.

This rule covers two separate subjects. First, helping gentiles. Second, making some sort of donation whenever asked. But the two go together, since the beggar going from door to door is as apt to be a gentile as a Jew. The point is that you have the obligation to help everyone in the community, not only Jews. The welfare of all, the "peace" in the sense of wholeness, depends on it. The Jewish community has a record extending through millenia: Jews give to all in need.

The case of the beggar going from door to door brings us back, too, to the matter of respect. You cannot turn the person away. Even if you have little or nothing to give, you do what you can. The person is on the line. Asking is hard, shameful, humiliating. It can be made tolerable and honorable—by you. If you respond in a friendly way, giving what you can, the one who asks gets back what has been given: dignity, personhood (so to speak). *What* you give matters less than *that* you give.

The law's reference to a dry fig, of course, alerts us to a task we have yet to face: how to translate this law into our own times. Our problems must be met in a world in which, if you gave a dry fig, you would not help much. That obvious fact raises the problem.

FOR OUR COMMUNITY

North American Jews have a proud record of participation in civic organizations of all kinds. We cannot be accused of neglecting non-Jewish poor or any programs of general importance, whether the United Fund or the Red Cross, the local museum of art or symphony orchestra, the local college or university, the local hospitals and homes for the aged. Here Jewish law indicates that such behavior is actually required of us—good citizenship is an obligation.

6. *The Giving Is What Matters*

If the poor person comes forth and asks for enough to satisfy, and if the giver cannot afford so much, the giver may donate as much as can be afforded. How much? In the highest fulfillment of this mitzvah, as much as one-fifth of the donor's possessions; in average performance of the mitzvah, up to one-tenth of the donor's possessions; less than this indicates the donor is a person with an evil eye. Always, a person must be sure of giving no less than one-third of a *shekel* per year. One who gives less has not fulfilled the mitzvah at all. Even a poor person who lives entirely from charity must give charity to another poor person.

The law makes provision for gradations of giving, relative to the proportion of one's property or income that is donated to tzedakah—from a fifth to a tenth, but no less. There is a fixed minimum, set at a very modest sum. Everyone must give some minimal sum. Even the poor must come up with it. So the law constructs a web of engagement in tzedakah, in which all participate, however modestly. The main thing is that everyone gives. Thus the community becomes concrete and fully realized. It is, in fact, the mark that the residents of a given place regard themselves as a community, as responsible beyond themselves.

The rule may seem puzzling, however, since it has two separate messages, one at the beginning and end, the second in the middle. It starts by saying you give as much as you can; and it ends by saying even the poor give as much as they can.

But in the middle, it tells how much you should give! Here too there is a balance between one thing and something else, between the fact that you give, and the amount that you give. The giving is what matters. Even a poor person must not be deprived of the honor and dignity of helping others.

Tzedakah is both a right and a privilege—to the giver. We are not whole and complete human beings unless we give. That is the fundamental affirmation of this stunning statement that a poor person must give to the poor. I cannot imagine a more profound and complete statement of Judaism than that simple one. Yet there is another half to the matter.

Giving must involve a *significant* contribution. The most generous is measured by the proportion of property donated to tzedakah: twenty percent. The average must be ten percent. There are religious groups, such as the Mormons, in which members tithe their income, before taxes. Jews are rightly proud of their philanthropic record, yet it would be difficult to claim that Jews in the main give ten percent of their gross income to tzedakah in all its forms—though, to be sure, being Jewish may well be expensive overall. In any event, the balance between the two principles—everyone has the dignity of giving, but there is a minimum that is expected—is clear.

FOR OUR COMMUNITY

The law before us indicates that it is the responsibility of the community to set a standard for giving. Tzedakah is not a matter of whim or how one likes the solicitors or distributors of charitable funds. It is a matter of duty, of mitzvah. Accordingly, organizations set membership dues. Federations and other philanthropic drives long ago ceased to publicize the amounts people give. That policy is enlightened. At the same time, there must be clear standards for giving, and these must be divorced from the convenience of donors. But they must also be realistic.

The primary goal for our day is that everyone give. A set minimum, a scale of giving, must be established. But alongside is the goal of massive participation.

Any community in which a few give the funds and dispose of them is not strong, however much money it raises. A community in which everyone gives something and has a voice in how the money is allocated is an effective and enduring community, no matter how little it raises. The law sets a minimum so that everyone may give with self-respect. For our context, the emphasis must be on tzedakah as the mode of Jewish identification (not the only mode, but a very prominent one), and we want all Jews to identify Jewishly. Each Jew's individual contribution is seen as important, hence each Jew is regarded as precious.

Laws Concerning Collection of Tzedakah

The equation of tzedakah creates a balance between donor and recipient, need and obligation. The recipient must enjoy respect and esteem. Dignity is paramount. Poverty is a condition, not a curse. The poor person must not be shamed and must not feel shame. The donor, on the other side, gets while giving: honor, self-esteem, the sense of doing duty and carrying out obligation. At the same time, the donor must supply not only funds but also respect, esteem, honor. The donor gives what the donor possesses—not money alone, but position, standing, dignity. There is the equation, a delicately poised balance between opposites.

We approach now the most practical matter: how to collect the money in a world of jealousy and selfishness. People are jealous of those in positions of power and of honor. So the ones who bear responsibility for actually doing the work of tzedakah enjoy the protection of the law. People do not naturally give away what they have. They must be subject to the requirements of the law as well. Collecting money is, quite evidently, the most practical matter of tzedakah.

1. *Collecting Tzedakah*

> In every city in which Israelites have settled, they are required to appoint from among their number, well-known and trustworthy persons to act as collectors of charity funds, to go around collecting from the people each Friday. These collectors should demand from each person what is proper for that one to give and what amount has been assessed to that person; and they should distribute the money each Friday, giving each poor person enough money for seven days. This is what is referred to as the "charity fund."
>
> Likewise, they must appoint others to collect each day, from every courtyard, bread and other foodstuffs, fruits, or money from anyone who is willing to make a voluntary offering at that time. They should distribute these the same evening among the poor, giving of them to each poor person in amounts sufficient for the day. This is what is referred to as the "charity tray."
>
> We have never seen nor heard of an Israelite community without a charity fund. With regard to the charity tray, there are some places where it is customary, and some where it is not. Presently, the popular custom is for the collectors of the charity fund to go around every day, and then distribute the proceeds every Friday.

This law takes up where the last one in the preceding chapter leaves off, with the notion that individuals become a community through the shared labor of tzedakah. The first thing we notice is that those in charge of collecting funds for tzedakah must be people of standing. It is an honor to them; and an honor to the community. In the end, this talmudic saying must be memorized by every member of every nominating committee of every Jewish organization and institution in the United States and Canada:

It is not the position that honors the person, but the person that honors the position.

In consonance, the law requires the people in charge of tzedakah to be well-known and trustworthy. They do the work routinely. They come with demands, not merely as beggars for beggars. They symbolize something for us all.

We notice, further, how to arrange the soup kitchen, here called a "charity tray." That, too, is worked out by community representatives. Finally, the law states a certainty—*a Jewish community that does not provide for tzedakah is unknown.* That is the fact today, too. It is, indeed, the definition of what it means to constitute a Jewish community. Whatever else people do, if they do not do tzedakah, they are not a Jewish community.

To people active in Federation and other communal work, this comes as no surprise. The language in which it is expressed may be different. The procedures are pretty much the same. The "workers" for the "Federation"—in the setting of the law of Judaism—are to be trustworthy and well-known. That is because others must accept their demands. What makes the "collectors of charity funds" authoritative is the moral authority they have earned in the community. People listen to them because they have earned respect, the right to make demands. These positions rest upon honor, and they enhance the honor of the ones who fill them.

Once again, Jewish law presupposes that the one who raises the money also bears responsibility for spending it. The poor must receive what they need from week to week. For more immediate needs, too, the community makes provision, on an everyday basis.

The observation at the end, that Maimonides has never seen or heard of a Jewish community lacking a fund for tzedakah, brings us down to our own day. Whatever else Jews do or do not do together, they always and invariably engage in the work of tzedakah. A Jew is someone who participates in tzedakah—and that is the beginning and end of the matter.

FOR OUR COMMUNITY

This law speaks most directly to the nominating committees of all Jewish organizations and institutions. They must seek people whom others will respect. This applies especially to the choice of officers for the community at large. Commonly, the nominating committee emerges with the message, "That was the only possible choice." But when a community lives under the representation of "the only possible choice" it is a sentence of, if not death, then resentment. A good president must be trustworthy not only in money matters but in Jewish values. Such a person must set an example for giving but also for caring. Since Federations and communal organizations endure through the work of the professionals—the social workers, the executives—the president must know how to work with people who know more about how to get the job done, but require guidance in precisely what job needs doing. The mark of a good president is the effectiveness of the professionals.

Most organizations provide a series of "steps" through which leadership is achieved and leaders are trained. But the president still must be chosen, as Maimonides says, for trust and repute. We are required to respond to leadership, and therefore to care deeply about what sort of persons are placed in positions of speaking for, and to, us all.

2. *Who Collects Tzedakah?*

Contributions to the charity fund must be collected

jointly by two persons, and a demand for money may not be addressed to the community by any less than two collectors. The funds collected, then, may be entrusted for safekeeping to one person. The charity fund must be distributed by three persons, inasmuch as it is analogous to money involved in a civil action, and funds sufficient for a week for each poor person must be provided.

This law carries forward the basic philosophy of the preceding one. The main point is that two people approach each donor, three people (at a minimum) decide on the allocation of funds. Why two? Because they represent the community, rather than any individual within the community. Why three? Because, as Maimonides says, the community is obligated to the poor. Hence, a claim on the funds of the community is a legal one. It must be adjudicated by a court. The three members of the "allocations committee" act as a court, dispensing public property as they do. And a court, in Jewish law, is made up of at least three judges. The rest follows.

The notion of "two on one" will not surprise anyone active in Federation work. What is striking is the reason cited by the law. The transaction of tzedakah, we know full well, is not merely a matter of whim. It is a duty. The community does not beg for tzedakah from the individual Jew. The community demands tzedakah, as much as the government demands taxes. The Jew is responsible to participate; to "give," then, is not really the correct verb. The Jew no more "gives" tzedakah than the citizen "gives" income taxes to the federal government. You pay your taxes because you must.

If you give tzedakah because it is your duty, then you do so for the right reason. The law is so framed as to express that fact. The claim for tzedakah comes from two people, because it is a demand—in the name, by the authority, of the Jewish community. True, once the funds are collected, one person may be allowed to hold them. That is not an issue of value or symbol. But at least three must divide the money. Again the stress is on the full responsibility and power of the community, three acting for the whole. It is not possible to make a rule more fully to express the basic principle at hand: tzedakah is an obligation, and it is communal, not private.

FOR OUR COMMUNITY

It is as if the law were speaking directly to fund-drive workers. In raising funds, they must see themselves as representatives of everybody. The imminent danger is that they allow fund raising to become a personal transaction, among friends. The concept of tzedakah would thus remain unfulfilled. Charity would be given, but righteousness would not be done.

As to allocations, we may move a step beyond the law as it is now stated. It is one thing for allocations committees to do the actual division of funds. But should there not be community discussion, prior to committe meetings, to determine priorities from one year to the next? Why not call public meetings for this purpose? If the organizations and institutions are "the organized Jewish community"—and they are—then it is time for the law to find expression in the light of this fact. So the "three persons" of the law should stand for town meetings of all concerned people. Let different viewpoints come to full expression. Let the processes of compromise and negotiation and voting run their course. The communities are made up of diverse people and interests. Why stifle that fact? Why not draw strength from the collaboration of individuals?

3. *How to Deal with Refusal*

The one who refuses to give charity, or gives less than is proper for that person, must be compelled to give by the court, and must be flogged for disobedience until she or he gives as much as the court estimates is due.

The court may even sieze property, taking what it is proper for that person to give. Indeed, a person may pawn goods in order to give charity, even on the eve of Sabbath.

The chain of reasoning remains unbroken. Just as a court disposes of community funds in payment of community obligations, so a court has power over the individual members of the community in collecting funds for tzedakah. The court sets the minimum, and the court then imposes civil or corporal penalties— flogging being a penalty that a Jewish court might inflict. The court may simply enter into the resident's property and take what is owing. If ready cash was not in hand, the court might take a pledge and pawn it, in order to realize what was owing. These are strong measures.

Jewish law is framed for a community able to exercise authority over its members. Accordingly, the law makes provision for taking what the community has coming, just as does the tax collector. The law presupposes courts of law, able to enforce obligations. Just as you take out a loan to pay taxes, so you may have to borrow money to provide tzedakah. So we are not dealing with good will, let alone with whim. We are dealing with dignity, honor, duty, citizenship: a community able to carry out its responsibilities.

The Federations and organizations today come with rightful claims. Lacking the power of courts, they exercise only moral authority. But most of the things we do result from the respect of our duties. We cannot be coerced to obey the law if we do not believe in the law. So the Jewish community today must conduct itself in such a way as to lay claim upon moral authority. That can be power enough. The alternative is not to go to court, but to appeal to emotions, to coerce through powerful personalities, to manipulate opinion through slogans and other devices of public relations. These devices leave the authority of the community in the power of sentiment and whim. Over the long run it is better to work through establishing an ongoing claim of duty to respond to authority based on conviction, that is, as I said, moral authority. For that purpose, people of conviction, standing, and conscience—even if it be difficult—must be included, not excluded.

FOR OUR COMMUNITY

A code of law turns wisdom and experience into a norm. What we have to do is collect the insight of organizations and institutions into a code of experience: How shall we deal with the people who will not give? First, of course, we have to make sure there is a serious approach to all potential givers, and, for the Federations for example, that means all the Jewish families in a given locality. The very act of solicitation is an approach of Jewry even to those Jews distant from Jewish life. It is an engagement with whatever Judaism the apparently assimilated Jew is apt to have. It should be regarded as an educational encounter.

What the inactive Jew must learn is that she or he is important and cannot be spared. The insistence must be upon the renewed engagement with Israel, the Jewish people. For Jews far from the community, tzedakah is probably the only Jewish deed that is possible. But, if done, it can be enough—for starters. Therefore we must continue to approach and never to reproach the inactive Jew. In this regard, all Jewish organizations have an equal contribution to make, since in seeking members, or in seeking to make active members of inactive ones, organizations may reach out in ways that other solicitors of funds cannot. We must keep asking. We must show ourselves to care deeply about every Jew.

4. *How to Deal with Excessive Generosity*

A munificent person who gives to charity beyond what

**he or she can afford, or who denies self in order to give
to the collector of charity so that she or he will not be
put to shame, should not be asked for contributions to
charity. Any fund raiser who humiliates such a person
by demanding charity of that person will surely be held
accountable for it, as it is stated, *I will punish all that
oppress them.***

This law deals with the opposite case from the foregoing. Now
we consider one who gives more than can be afforded. Or denies
his or her own needs. A person likely to give too much must not
be approached. That is the law. Everyone is supposed to give a
fair share. But just as no one may give less than is owed, so no
one may be permitted to give at the sacrifice of real personal
needs. The upshot of such giving would be that the person
would need to draw on tzedakah. That we cannot permit.

Thus, the one who will not give has a counterpart. There is a
person who wants to give more than a fair share. Such a person
may not be exploited; and it is again a question of balance.

A fine insight into human nature is before us. There are
those who feel good or important when they give. Giving is,
after all, a great virtue. It also is, at one and the same time, a
vice. For to give is to dominate. It is to purchase something one
does not have coming. If everyone gives a reasonable amount
(ten percent, we recall) and one person wants to give forty or
fifty percent of his or her entire wealth and income, that creates
an imbalance that the community may not exploit. Such a person must be held in check, as much as the one who refuses to
give at all. The reason is different. For one, the welfare of the
community requires all to give a fair share. But by the same
token, the order and balance of the community require that no
person dominate.

So the purpose of the present law is subtle. It is not merely
to avoid embarrassing a person who is too generous, or to pre-
vent the humiliation of the one who wants to give more than is
really suitable. The law will not permit the possibility of the

"big giver." The reason is stated in one way: not humiliating such a person. But there is a further consideration, I think, to be taken into account. It is to distinguish between having people do their share, on the one side, and allowing them to do far more than their share, on the other.

FOR OUR COMMUNITY

At issue is what we are supposed not to do. Jewish organizational life must never present a frowning picture to the Jewish people. The doors must always be open. No one may be put to shame, for giving too little, for giving not at all. The approach must always be made with dignity and honor: this is our duty, this is our opportunity to serve. If someone does not give one year, we come back the next—with good will all the time. That is why we do not take every penny we can get in any one year, as the law says. The "sacrificial giving" in the annual "emergency" or "crisis" produces not only boredom, it also embarrasses people who take to heart the rhetoric of the annual campaign. So there are two separate problems: the one who gives too little, the one who gives too much. But the underlying question is the same in both instances: embarrassing people. The law requires us to avoid this through a sensitivity toward others and forethought as to what particular community members are inclined to do.

5. *The Status of a Pledge*

The giving of charity may be considered [legally] within the category of "vows." Therefore, when a person says, "I obligate myself to give [a certain amount] in charity," or "This [specific amount] is set aside for charity," the obligation is to give it to the poor immediately. If the donor tarries, it is a transgression of the commandment, *You shall not be slack to pay it,* inasmuch as it is within the donor's power to dispense the [given sum] immediately, and poor people are readily available. If there are no poor in that vicinity, the donor may set aside the amount and leave it until poor people are available.

If the donor stipulates that the charity is to be given only when a poor person is found, the amount vowed need not be set aside [in advance].

Similarly, if the donor stipulates at the time the vow is made or promises the free-will offering that the charity collectors are to be free to use part of the amount or combine that amount with others for conversion into [larger] coin, they are permitted to do so.

The proof text in this law states the obvious: once you make a pledge, you have to pay it promptly. The need is pressing. Still, the law permits a pledge to be conditional. If you pledge that when it is needed, you will give money, you are allowed to do things just that way. If you specify in your pledge that the people in charge of the funds may dispose of your money in the way most advantageous to the cause of the poor or needy, that is a valid pledge, too.

The main point is if someone promises to give money for tzedakah, that constitutes a vow. In Jewish law, a vow is binding. It is made to Heaven, that is to say, if you take a vow, you give your word to God. Thus, one who pledges money and does not pay up is not merely a burden and a disgrace. Such a person is also a sinner. Jewish law in the end addresses questions not only of the here and now, but also of eternity. In this-worldly terms, one may commit a felony; in other worldly terms, a felony is a sin. It remains true that the one who pledges money and does not pay is a fourflusher and a bluffer. But in the setting of Judaism, such a person is committing an offense against Heaven.

There is a social aspect to this problem as well. If a person pledges but then does not pay promptly, the poor suffer. People plan on the anticipated funds; the poor must be fed, housed, and clothed. When a pledge is allowed to lapse, clearly, others must make up the sum. But even if the donor does not pay promptly, the funds prove less useful later. The poor need now—not when it is convenient for the donor. The purpose of tzedakah is to deal with pressing needs. Tzedakah postponed, so to speak, is tzedakah denied. For both religious and social considerations, the pledge—a vow—is urgent, an account to be settled promptly.

FOR OUR COMMUNITY

The law requires that we keep our word. The word of a good person is a bond. The law views us as people of honor, people who respect themselves. There is nothing more to be said.

6. *Schnorring*

The one who presses others to give charity and moves them actually to do so gains a reward greater than the reward of the one who personally gives charity, as it is stated, *And the work of righteousness shall be peace.*

The proof text, drawn from the prophet Isaiah, is the main point here. Since the word for "righteousness" and the word for "charity" are one and the same, the text is taken to mean, "The work of tzedakah shall be peace." The one who does that work— who sits in the chairs, so to speak—is the one who brings peace to our community. Now the word "peace," as we know, stands for wholeness and completeness. The work of tzedakah is to make the community whole and complete—and that is the point. No one can doubt it, since, we now realize, when people carry on the labors of tzedakah, they form the Jewish community at the very same time they are fulfilling the obligations and responsibilities of the community. Tzedakah is the one thing that all Jews in any given town or city have in common. Without tzedakah, there is nothing they are apt to do collectively and unanimously.

Those humbly working for the campaigns give up not only time but also themselves, their own prestige. When they call on a potential donor, they are asking for something. The potential donor may well suppose that, in time to come, she or he may ask for something as well. The most honorable Jewish calling is *schnorring* (Yiddish for "seeking funds," often used derisively), as this law makes explicit.

Schnorring is of greater merit than merely giving, since when you go to someone and ask for something, you put yourself on the line. If the potential donor refuses, the refusal is not of the philanthropy, the "cause." It is personal: *you* are turned down. Some fortunate people have the inner peace to accept disappointment and denial. Most do not, myself included.

The *schnorrer* ("seeker of funds") who works for the sake of Heaven enjoys the highest reward. The schnorrer risks most; and, if truth be told, gets the least: mere satisfaction at sustaining not only the poor, but the community as a whole. The community cannot endure without the schnorrer.

Considering the possibilities inherent for upset and disappointment, it may be difficult to see how Isaiah can promise the exact opposite, peace. Yet the meaning is this: if the work of tzedakah succeeds, if the schnorrer does the work well, then, in truth, the community is made whole, enjoys peace in the rich and full sense of the Hebrew term, *shalom*.

FOR OUR COMMUNITY

The Jewish merchant who keeps a *pushke* (Yiddish: collection box) on the counter, the Hadassah member with her constant calls for donations, the day shool people knocking on one door after another—these are the heroes of our community. The women and men who attend committee and board meetings, who sit for endless hours listening to speeches, and who come back for more—these are people who keep Jewry alive and working. They do the work of righteousness, tzedakah; and they bring peace, shalom, to the community. Those who labor year after year, whether honored or not honored, whether recognized or not recognized, tending the vineyard of charitable organizations and institutions—these are the ones who make it all work. To them, all honor! What we are required to be is a people, one people. Those who draw us together in a common cause—they make us one.

Are These Laws Relevant?

People pay ritual courtesies. They say hello when they scarcely know you. They ask how you are when they don't want to know the answer. Among Jews, it is expected that people will respect "Torah" and champion the words of Torah and the Torah itself. Then they will do pretty much whatever they want anyhow. I don't mean they will say "You shall not murder," then go out and commit murder. I mean they will affirm that "The Torah is the guide to life," and then run Jewish institutions and organizations without asking what guidance they might find in Judaism.

True, critics might make them feel guilty. But it seldom occurs that most Jewish organizational and communal leaders, whether professionals or others, study Maimonides' laws of giving to the poor and then organize and define their programs in accord with these laws.

Now we have an ample collection of sayings about how holy it is to "give to tzedakah." The laws in the previous chapters, the verses of Scripture relating to tzedakah, the numerous stories and sayings in the Talmud—all of these form a great treasury. The treasury provides what people want. They do not wish to be told what to do, by which I mean, they are not looking for laws. What they want is proof for what they already do or what they already plan to do. That is to say, they are looking for proofs, for authority, for someone old and dead to quote on behalf of what the living want to do anyhow. The laws and sayings validate because they provide proof for the self-evident. The alternative would be for the laws and sayings to loom up as problems because they exercise authority—a very different circumstance.

Proof Texts and Pretexts

Now, if you are looking for proof texts, what a marvelous treasure trove we have just examined! I left the best for the last: the statement that if you go and ask someone for money, it is better than if you give the money yourself. In context, that saying is part of a larger world view, an encompassing theory of what tzedakah means and of how tzedakah defines us as Jews. We shall dwell on that point in just a moment. But standing by itself, that statement makes wonderful material for a pep talk to campaign workers (as well it should). So it will be quoted by itself and be honored and revered, because it proves what people want to prove.

The real issue before us is whether we can learn anything from Jewish law. The reason it is an issue is simple. In searching the sources for texts that prove what we have already decided is true—hence, proof texts—we are not interested in the law at all. We want only to buttress our ideas or merely our rhetoric with the authority of the law. Since people know the difference between a text and a proof text, they are not apt to respond to a proof text. It is part of the flood of Jewish words rushing past their ears, at best a way of watering dried-up emotions.

When we truly ask whether the laws are relevant to the world we know, therefore, the question is hardly commonplace. It is obvious that the laws are relevant, because from them we may pick out numerous proof texts. It is self-evident that the laws cover matters of policy and practice entirely familiar in today's world. So it is easy to see that "back then" they also had to worry about the one who would not give, or the one who wanted to give too much. In these matters, the laws are self-evidently relevant. But such points of contact with our own world are trivial and essentially beside the point.

The question facing us is whether we can learn from these laws a better way of understanding ourselves. That is, when we uncover the basic principles of the laws, the view of what we are and what we should be that is expressed within the details of the law, do we learn something helpful? Or are the basic principles of the law so remote, on the one hand, or so banal and obvious, on the other, as to be essentially irrelevant?

1. *The Laws Are Irrelevant*

No more than a stockpile of stunning proof texts, the laws are hardly relevant in fundamental ways. Let us review the laws and so list, in some detail, the suppositions or facts in no way pertinent to the world we occupy.

The fundamental concern of the laws of tzedakah is for persons; and the situation involves a donor and a recipient. The eight degrees of alms-giving emphasize the value of the donor's not knowing the identity of the recipient. For us that is rather easy, since we send a check to an office. Following that, by passing through many committees and offices, the money we give reaches the person to be assisted. Accordingly, we could not know to whom we have given. Nor can the poor person know from whom specific monies have been received. There are, indeed, some philanthropic ventures which attempt to bridge the gap Jewish law wishes (for its reasons) to create. But Jewish law assumes a personal relationship generally absent in the conditions of tzedakah in which we do our work. Who cares, while writing out a check to the Federation or dues to ORT, whether we are smiling or scowling?

What has been said in general obviously applies in detail. People who deal with Jewish agencies of tzedakah rarely have to worry about selling, or not selling, their houses, fields, and vineyards, in the rainy season. The details of the phrasing of the law scarcely relate to our time.

Indeed, the very supposition of a settled community of people at essentially the same economic level hardly makes sense. The theory of how a person becomes poor seems to be that there is a sudden turn in one's fortunes. The poor person is commonly supposed to have once had, and now lost, money and property. It is a temporary condition, or one which, in any event, may be improved. The notion of a permanent underclass of people requiring perpetual support is scarcely before us. The further consideration of all of the other works of tzedakah for which we bear responsibility, beyond feeding the poor, is nearly alien to the whole of the law we have considered.

The law, in its concern for the dignity of the poor, indicates that we provide for the poor in accord with their station in life. Once again, we notice that being poor is an unhappy accident, not a condition. Hence, if a person had a horse and herald, but lost those perquisites of wealth, we are instructed to provide a horse and a herald. It is necessary, therefore, to differentiate between this poor person and that one; and the criterion is the prior status of each. There is hardly any limit on what a poor person may demand of the community. The community need not restore what has been lost. Yet the community is required to restore the standing that has been diminished.

We notice the fundamental irrelevance of the laws, further, when we provide for immediate meals, no matter what. True, under certain circumstances, the community may have to maintain soup kitchens. But this area of the law is not usually relevant to our situation.

Furthermore, the notion that the poor near at hand take precedence over the poor far away may make sense in an age of limited travel and slow communications. But now that we live in a global village, how can we say with certainty who is near and who is far? The Jewish community has many concerns, and some of them involve Jews in distant places. True, we must provide for our own. But who is not our own? Certainly we have to take care of relatives and townsfolk. But others are at least as near as these: as near as today's newspaper. Jews are not isolationists.

Likewise, it would be difficult to find a less auspicious precept than the notion that we should encourage begging from door to door. I cannot imagine anything more repulsive and embarrassing than having the poor knock on our doors and ask for a contribution. The danger to the community need hardly be specified; people are frightened as it is. Again, despite the fine example of the Mormons in tithing their income before taxes, still, outside of the range of tzedakah, there are many things we support which lay claim upon our income.

The personalization of dispensing tzedakah finds its counterpart in the personal and individual way in which funds are collected. It is well and good to point to the notion of "two on one," that the community should be represented by more than one individual when charity is being solicited. But should people go once a week to collect money for tzedakah, as the law prescribes, they are not apt to find a warm welcome. In general, we do not relish knocks on the door, either from the poor, or from solicitors. We see such intrusions as an invasion of privacy.

We need hardly point to the notion of maintaining tables of food in poor neighborhoods, let alone the notion that we might be required to drop off a can of peas at a local poverty center.

Nor are we likely to see the necessity of having three people represent the community by dropping off a check from the Federation or one of its agencies to the needy. It only takes a postage stamp. Nor can we concur with the law that states three people constitute an adequate committee to decide on the allocation of communal funds. Thirty would seem a small number, in a sizable community; three would appear to be plutocracy.

True, campaign workers may wish they could go to court to collect a donation, all the more so to impose a donation of the size they think a person can and should give. But that particular law—not to mention the detail of the court's seizing the unwilling donor's property!—speaks of a world we can scarcely imagine even in fantasy. As to the "big giver," the one who endangers his or her own economic status in order to fulfill the mitzvah of tzedakah, rarely do campaign workers face the problem of refusing a gift because the person who gives it really cannot afford to do so. Whether or not they would refuse such a gift, we cannot say. It is not an everyday problem.

True, the unpaid pledge is as much a problem now as it was eight hundred years ago when Maimonides' code of Jewish law was drafted. But the rest of the law addresses problems remote from our experience. And, finally, the idea that the one who presses others to give is due a "greater reward" than the one who gives alms may be noble and heartening. But try to persuade the donors—I mean, the (roughly) ten percent of the givers who provide (roughly) ninety percent of the funds!

Here and there we note valid ideas expressed in the law. There are details we find appealing, points relevant to our tasks. But in the main the Jewish laws we have examined speak to a different world. They address person-to-person giving. We live not in personal communities, but in a world of impersonal institutions. The laws assume involvement of individuals. We do our business in groups. The laws of tzedakah are formulated for retail, so to speak, but we live in an age of wholesale.

The world has changed from a time in which people pretty much knew one another. There is now a theory of poverty that makes provision for something other than bad luck. Tzedakah today is systematic, well-organized, impersonal. More kinds of activities are undertaken in the name of tzedakah than ever before. Federations and welfare funds, for instance, take responsibility for a far larger world than the one of poor people. There are the elderly and infirm, the emotionally and physically handicapped, the displaced and the oppressed. Everything has changed. Nothing is the same. The laws are irrelevant.

2. *The Laws Are Relevant*

The details of the law do not address our world, or many other worlds before our own day. But we have much to learn from the laws both directly and indirectly.

The world portrayed in the laws presents us a picture quite strange to our eyes: a world in which tzedakah is personal and individual. The reason Jewish law makes the points it does, lays emphasis on the treatment of the poor person, for instance, is simple. The law speaks to a world in which people meet and know one another. The great institutions of society known to us—bureaucracies, organizations, corporations, and the like—stand between each of us and the things we wish to accomplish. But we must have them since, in the end, they accomplish the things we wish to do. So in order to get things done, we have to have a Jewish National Fund, an Anti-Defamation League, a Federation—organized philanthropies. If each of us went out in search of a poor person, we should do no good (not to mention, turn ourselves into clowns). We do not want beggars at our doors; beggars do not want to beg. We do want to help people.

Still, it does us no harm to contemplate a legal system in which the donor is still a person, the recipient still an object of concern and dignity. True, it is not as donors that we play a role in the work of the agencies and institutions of tzedakah. They stand for us, as much as if we stood out in the forefront of social work, or programs to improve the life of the poor or the needy in the State of Israel, in the Soviet Union, here at home. Accordingly, the details of the law may be irrelevant. But the main principles are instructive and important. These are what pertains to our world, why the study of the Jewish law of tzedakah is relevant.

The first of Maimonides' eight degrees of charity is as fresh today as it was eight hundred years ago. It is better to lend, for purposes of investment, than to give. It is better to find work for the poor than to let the poor go out to beg. But what about the other seven stages: respect for the dignity of the poor person, the anonymity of the donor and recipient?

When I contemplate the popular attitude of North American Jews visiting the Land of Israel, looking for the trees they planted, telling Israelis about how hard they work for the United Jewish Appeal, I find it difficult to agree that these degrees of Maimonides are irrelevant. On the contrary, the attitude of "Lord and Lady Bountiful" bestowing mercies with condescension, has not passed away from the world with the advent of large organizations of tzedakah. I do not mean to say we should not record generosity. I mean to say the stages of almsgiving have much to teach us.

The acute contemporaneity of the rules on how to treat the poor in general is striking. In an age in which we ask poor people to "divest" themselves of their television sets to receive welfare support, it is still important to hear that we should not force the sale of assets. At a time when we provide only minimal necessities for the poor, and sometimes even less, it is healthy to be told to buy the poor a horse to ride. When there are high walls between the needy and the money they need, it is not irrelevant to study a law emphasizing the importance of quick and prompt sustenance.

When the extended family is no more and the nuclear family itself is weak, it is urgent to be reminded that the support of relatives, not even close at hand, takes priority. Nor in a Jewish community centered on what happens overseas does it do any harm to consider a law that says the poor at home take precedence.

The law that requires us not to say no to the poor is easily translated into the rule that, however little you give, you must give. Too much emphasis is laid on how much, too little on how intended. Given the generally modest levels of support for tzedakah, it does no harm to be told Jewish law demands we give ten percent of our gross income to tzedakah. I cannot, in truth, point to a single irrelevant law in the entire canon of Jewish rules of tzedakah.

Experienced men and women do not have to turn to Jewish law for helpful hints on how to solicit funds. But they may gain much by reflecting on the basic attitudes expressed through the law. For the main point throughout is to emphasize the dignity of the transaction of tzedakah. The prinicpal fact is that the person who asks for money is to be honored. The one who gives it is to be respected for doing what is duty and obligation. But there is no need to exaggerate the honor and glory of the donation. To the contrary, the transaction must be among equals: solicitor of funds, donor, recipient.

The solicitors work in pairs, because this symbolizes the fact that the transaction has legal standing, in the name not of a private person but of "we," that is, the Jewish community. The two stand for all. The one who will not give cannot be compelled to do so in court. But the community need not stand idly by. It should begin to develop modes of dealing with people who wish to participate in community life but who will not perform their obligations. Citizens pay taxes.

Jews bear their fair share of the responsibilities of the whole. But the community, for its part, must respect the individual. Leaders must lead, not lord it over people. Persuasion and open discussion are the tools of community. The basic attitude must be one of mutual trust. Without that, nothing else is worth attempting.

The "too-generous" donor has to be kept in line. This sort,

in the law, is the one who gives more than he or she can afford. The pledge must be presented as a moral, as well as a legal, obligation. Above all, the one who works for the community— the campaign workers, the professional staff—must enjoy the respect and esteem accorded by the law.

In short, in reviewing the main points of the law, I have shown that each one is acutely relevant to our own situation.

Where We Stand

The laws are both irrelevant and exquisitely relevant. We see in them details that are jarring. These derive from a context far removed from ours. Yet we perceive in them an insight into proper attitudes and opinions, notions of dignity and worth. Beneath the surface of the structure of laws we find a deeper layer of rules on caring and sharing.

Maimonides need not be the only codifier of law. For we today have the intelligence and standing to codify laws operative in our own communities, to create a "book" of accepted practice. The process of forming Jewish law is continuous, from Sinai to us; and, if we succeed, for yet future generations. For this purpose, we turn now from *halakhah*, law, to *aggadah*, lore. For this task, we now seek the deep structure, the heart of the matter: What does Judaism have to say about tzedakah?

From the Ordinary
to the Holy

The laws speak of this world, things we do and do not do under ordinary circumstances. Left only with the eight stages of tzedakah, and the twelve laws we have examined, you would miss the point of it all. For the laws merely hint at the beliefs and ideals that stand behind them. We are able to tease out of the code statements on the values expressed in it, such as the importance of dignity, responsibility, duty. To seek those statements in a fully articulated and accessible form, we turn from the legal literature to the other kind of literature of Judaism.

That other kind of writing is called, in Hebrew, *aggadah*, generally translated as "narrative." You are probably familiar with the term from the name of the prayer book used at the Passover Seder, the *Haggadah*, the "narrative" of the course of the Seder. Aggadah may be rendered, in a more general way, as "lore." Included are stories and sayings which contain or directly express fundamental beliefs. As we have seen in the counterpart, legal literature or halakhah, beliefs and ideals take the form of instructions on how to act. So what one says in theory, the other states in practice. The lore, or aggadah, and the law, or halakhah, together express Judaism: faith and deed, conviction and action.

Faith? Leave Me Out!

Now, for the so-called "nonreligious" Jews, talk of faith and conviction is hardly welcome. Such Jews take the view that long ago they lost interest in, or in fact rejected, religion in general, not just Judaism in particular. That does not mean they wish to avoid being good and loyal Jews. The contrary is the case. It means they do not wish to be synagogue Jews. More commonly, if they join synagogues, it is a mere formality. Given the acres of empty pews on important religious occasions in the synagogue, we have to regard the so-called "nonreligious" Jews as very many indeed.

Ironically for the Jew to whom Judaism is, at best, a matter of occasion and routine, Judaism cannot regard such Jews as "nonreligious" or "secular." From the viewpoint of the great authoritative sources of Judaism, every Jew remains "Israel," a member of the holy people, a descendant of Abraham and Sarah. The Torah confronts every Jew equally. Through the Torah God speaks to us, whether or not we choose to listen. These are simple affirmations, uniform throughout the Judaic tradition.

There is a further problem. The so-called "nonreligious" Jew engages in actions traditionally regarded as holy. Whatever the motive, the end result is this: precisely those deeds important to the Jew supposedly alien to Judaic piety loom up as critical in the religious life of Jews.

How can you be secular, if what you *do* is sacred? The question faces not only the professed atheists within the organizations of tzedakah—there are not so many of these. It accosts people active in synagogues, who wish to see their counterpart in Federations and other organizations as secular and themselves as religious. Still others, happily not many, regard their acts of worship and learning as expressions of piety, but the acts of tzedakah of community leaders not as expressions of piety. Or they may question the motives of communal leaders, saying they are looking for honor and public esteem, even while assuming the presidency of their synagogue or presuming to tell their rabbi what to do and not do. All of this trumpery, a circus of the Jewish spirit.

Any estrangement between the synagogue and the Federation bespeaks in this-worldly, political, and institutional terms, a deeper malady. The inner wholeness of Judaism is shattered. For people to think they can divide behavior from belief, is to wish to do what cannot be done. No one doubts you cannot be a good Jew if you say things but do not do things, but how can people think it is enough to do things without making sense of what is done and why?

Some, therefore, do acts of a sacred character, regarded through the whole of the Judaic tradition as paramount, while claiming these acts are merely secular. While others do acts of sacred character and regard Jews involved in the sacred work of tzedakah as somehow less authentic. Surely, the true sense of authenticity resides in the *meaning* of what is done, not merely in a given action. So it is the meaning of tzedakah that must now be examined.

Precisely how do the sages of Judaism view tzedakah? To answer, we shall focus on five stories—three on the theme of tzedakah and holiness; and two, which contradict one another, on the rewards of tzedakah. Our purpose now is to back up the claim that tzedakah is the highest act of piety we can do.

Tzedakah and Holiness

1. **Rabbi Hama, son of Rabbi Hanina, said, "What does Scripture mean when it states, *You shall walk behind the Lord your God?* Can a person truly walk behind the Divine Presence? Surely not! For is it not also stated that *the Lord is a devouring fire?* Rather [the verse must mean that] a person should imitate the righteous ways of the Holy One, the Blessed. Just as the Lord clothed the naked—as it is stated, *And the Lord God made for Adam and for his wife coats of skin and clothed them*—so, too, you must supply clothes for the naked poor. Just as the Holy One, the Blessed, visited the sick—as it is stated, *And the Lord appeared to Abraham who was sick by the oaks of Mamre*—so, too, you should visit the sick. Just as the Holy One, the Blessed, buried the dead—as it is stated, *And the Lord buried Moses in the valley*—so, too, you must bury the dead. Just as the Holy One, the Blessed, comforted mourners—as it is stated, *And it came to be after the death of Abraham that God blessed Isaac his son*—so, too, you should comfort mourners.**

The text before us unfolds in a very simple and logical way. First, we ask how we can go after God. Such a thing is not possible. What is possible is to follow the virtues of God, doing the deeds God does. Then these deeds are specified: clothing the naked, visiting the sick, burying the dead, comforting the mourners. These are acts of loving-kindness. They are also the things we do for one another to form a community of people who care. Each of the four deeds listed here are humble and ordinary. In the framework of tzedakah, there are equivalently humble and everyday "secular" deeds. After all, what is religious or holy about buying a suit of clothes for someone in need, or visiting someone in the hospital, or providing for a proper burial for someone lacking in funds or family, or expressing sympathy to someone who is bereaved? These are really ordinary and simple human actions. We do them naturally, not impelled by some deep religious conviction. Yet they form the sum and substance of the holy: they are what God does.

This conception, fetching in itself, is stunning in its implications. When, later on, you are confronted with the simple claim that in working for tzedakah and giving to tzedakah, you are "like God," you may not be puzzled or surprised. This is precisely the teaching of Torah. It is not propaganda, nor is it a bon mot offered up on a special occasion. It is Judaism's deepest conviction of what it is to be "like God."

When the story of the creation of man and woman speaks of them as made "in the image" of God, it invites precisely the interpretation of Rabbi Hama. We cannot imagine, he says, that being like God bears a material or physical meaning. It must mean that we do things God does—which is to say, acts of tzedakah.

If there is a problem in this story, it appears when we turn the story on its head. Are we godlike when we do these deeds, if we do not perform them in order to be like God? We *are*. For the story does not demand that we intend to imitate God by doing deeds of tzedakah. Thus, our view of our "secular" selves comes under inspection. If someone says you look like your father or your mother, or do things as they did and do them, that is a statement of fact, not choice. Along similar lines, whether you like it or not, when you do deeds of tzedakah, you are like God.

You may not see matters that way. Judaism, as represented here by Rabbi Hama, does. You may claim to be alien to the faith and foreign to the synagogue. Judaism does not care. If we take Rabbi Hama's story seriously, as we must, our view of the professedly secular Jew must change. For whatever such a Jew says, he or she acts in a way which is clear in the eyes of Judaism.

In these circumstances of faith, the burden of proof that one is truly secular lies upon the Jews who wish to deny they are religious while in fact doing the deeds of religion.

If you doubt that, turn it around. Can you claim to be religious if you say the words but do not act accordingly? If you pray but do not study Torah? Yes, you may claim to be religious, but will the claim stick? The deeply held conviction of Judaism that words without deeds are null has its counterpart here. Deeds without words matter. You are what you do. If you do the acts of faith, you may not—and need not—profess the faith. Your deeds speak for you.

FOR OUR COMMUNITY

At first glance the above may seem a bit of pedagogy, a convolution in reasoning. It is not. It is, instead, eye-opening. We are required to be "like God." Suddenly we discover that we are, though we have professed not to be. Now we apprehend that we must reflect on what we are. Are we not, all things considered, the sum total of our actions?

To a community like ours, so rich in doers but so reluctant to reflect, so full of achievement yet so hesitant to take thoughtful pride in achievement, the demand for self-reflection is difficult.

2. *Through the righteousness of charity, I shall behold Your face.* **Notice the immense power of tzedakah: For [the verse indicates that] a person who gives even a single small coin to the poor is deemed worthy to greet the Presence of God. In the material world, it is customary that a matron who wishes to be received by her king must fashion [for him] a suitable crown. And, by presenting this crown, which she brings to adorn him, [the matron becomes worthy of] beholding the face of the king. But a person needs only to give a small coin to the poor in order to greet the Presence of God.**

    Furthermore, why did David [author of the verse], see fit to discuss the power of tzedakah exclusively? So as to demonstrate that even the wicked, who have no

other virtues than the giving of tzedakah, are deemed worthy to greet the Presence of God.

The verse is read to mean, "I, through tzedakah, shall see Your face." Thus, if we give to tzedakah, we see God—just what the preceding statement wished to tell us. The rest follows. The proof text, drawn from the book of Psalms, makes possible the other statements before us.

In the setting of piety, a paradox appears. Tzedakah demands little and delivers much. But from our viewpoint what is important is in the second clause. *Tzedakah all by itself suffices.* "To greet the Presence of God" (that is, to see God's face) is represented at the outset as the supreme goal. To attain it, despite one's character in all other ways, one need only perform acts of tzedakah—it is a stunning affirmation. Let me raise two points.

First, notice that the rather general claim I made earlier about the ultimate value of tzedakah is here given the authority of the sages of Judaism. Were such a statement in their names not available, we should never have dared to make it. Many in Jewry hold the deep prejudice that people devoted to tzedakah but otherwise unimpressive, or genuinely bad, do not amount to much. That is a perfectly natural attitude of mind. Judaism rejects it. Perhaps we should be embarrassed at this view assigned to David. But it is present; it must be taken to heart. It is not a license to cheat or steal. It is a warning against self-righteousness among the good folk and an admonition about what is truly important.

Second, the remarkable statement that through tzedakah we see God has to be brought to earth. To translate that amazing allegation into deeds—hence, laws—we might legislate, "A man must wear a *kippah* (head-covering) at a Federation meeting; a woman must dress decorously." That would be a trivial example. The real challenge lies elsewhere. Since, in Judaism, we believe God is addressed through prayer, we come in a reverent spirit to *tefillot,* "services." Since we affirm that when we study the sacred writings of Judaism, we hear what God has revealed, that is, Torah, we assemble for study in a serious and respectful manner. How should we attend an organizational board meeting?

In context, the answer is clear. We must summon our best sense of ourselves, attend with idealism and high purpose. It would be an exaggeration to say that going to a committee meeting of an organization is equivalent to attending the synagogue for *Kol Nidre*. It would be an exaggeration, were it not for the astonishing statements in the passage before us!

FOR OUR COMMUNITY

Those who work in the labors of tzedakah are supposed to be good Jews, by definition. But another factor is operative, according to the text we have just encountered. Through the deeds of tzedakah, we make something deeper of ourselves. Tzedakah is a call to greatness. Spending your life in Jewish labors, in Jewish organizations and institutions—in the drudgery of it all—changes you. It becomes a way toward being a good Jew. Therein lies the challenge: at every turn you are called upon to see the yet-to-be-explored dimensions of your being Jewish.

3. **Rabbi Dostai, son of Rabbi Yannai, preached, Notice that the ways of flesh and blood are unlike the ways of God. The ways of flesh and blood are, if a person offers an expensive present to a king, it may be accepted or not. Furthermore, even if the present is accepted by the king, it is still uncertain whether the donor will be deemed worthy of an audience with the king. But the ways of the Holy One, the Blessed, are different. A person who gives but a small coin to the poor is deemed worthy to greet the Presence of God. For it is stated, *Through the righteousness of charity I shall behold Your face, and I shall be satisfied when I awake with Your likeness.***

Rabbi Eleazar once gave a small coin to a poor person, and afterwards prayed. Then he explained, It is written, *In the righteousness of charity I shall behold Your face.*

Here, too, the proof text we find in the foregoing passage applies, as is made explicit at the very end with the citation by Rabbi Eleazar. Once "the righteousness of charity" is read in the Hebrew as tzedakah, then every reference in Scripture to "righteousness" takes on a second, and deeper, meaning. The example comes before the proof text. If you tried to see a great officer of the government in ancient times, you would have to grease plenty of palms on the way in. Then you might or might not see the lord. But God, above all rulers, is available to you for a small coin. The irony and paradox contain both a bitter comment on the "real" world and a profound statement of the true reality of Israel, the Jewish people, in its life of tzedakah.

The conviction that when one attains merit through tzedakah, one beholds "the face of the Divine Presence" is already familiar. But Rabbi Eleazar's example is striking. He would first do a deed of tzedakah, then pray.

We should not imagine that the sages used the words before us merely to encourage people to do what they wanted them to do. The purpose was personal and immediate. The sages believed in tzedakah not as a means to an end, but as a mode of piety, equivalent to prayer. Once again, we must wonder whether it matters if one who performs tzedakah does not pray.

True, it matters by contemporary standards of Jewish piety. But people already have accepted what Judaism aforetimes could not: that Israel might ever cease to be Israel—that is, that a Jew could stop being a Jew. Judaism takes its position, through the ages. One affirmation in that position is before us. Tzedakah is a religious and only a religious deed. What difference does it make if some people who do tzedakah do not understand the full significance of what they do?

The sources before us say that it makes no difference at all. You can pray without perfect faith; all of us do, most of the time. Tzedakah is a deed—by definition, of perfect faith when rightly done.

FOR OUR COMMUNITY

In doing tzedakah, we perform a religious act. The text implies that tzedakah serves in this fashion as a model for other religious acts. The sage believed in tzedakah, but also in prayer; he did both. Few are the Jews who pray and do not give to tzedakah of some sort. But how numerous the Jews who separate tzedakah from other modes of Jewish expression!

The theme has been raised before, and we are now well aware that tzedakah is a fulfillment of the highest demands of Judaism. Tzedakah draws the community together, as virtually no other Jewish activity can. Having said this, it still remains to be said that those who perform the labors of tzedakah are equally required to take up and confront other questions raised by Judaism. If through tzedakah we stand at the pinnacle of Jewish life, surely we want to be certain there is a mountain beneath our feet.

The Reward of Tzedakah

1. **Rabbis Eliezer, Joshua, and Akiba went to the region of Antioch to make a collection for [needy] sages. There was there one Abba Yudan who had previously given generously to fulfill the mitzvah [of tzedakah], but had fallen upon hard times. When he saw the rabbis, Abba Yudan lost his composure and went directly to his home. His wife said to him, "Why do you look so sickly?" Abba Yudan replied, "The rabbis are here, and I am at a loss as to what I can do." His wife, even more concerned with tzedakah than her husband, said, "We still own one field. Go sell half of it, and make a contribution." This he went and did. The rabbis prayed**

for him and said, "Abba Yudan, may the Lord supply
your needs." Some days later, he went out to plow his
remaining half-field. And as he was plowing, the earth
opened up, causing his cow to slip and be injured. He
bent down to raise up the animal, and the Holy One, the
Blessed, opened his eyes and revealed a treasure hid-
den beneath the cow. Then Abba Yudan said, "It was
for my benefit that the cow broke its hoof."

Upon their return to Antioch, the rabbis inquired
after Abba Yudan. "How is Abba Yudan doing?" they
queried. And they were answered, "Who sees Abba
Yudan? He is surrounded by slaves. He is the Abba
Yudan of sheep, the Abba Yudan of asses, the Abba
Yudan of camels, the Abba Yudan of oxen!" Hearing
the rabbis had returned, Abba Yudan came out to greet
them. They asked him, "How is Abba Yudan doing?"
He answered, "Your prayer has borne fruit upon fruit."
They said, "Though others gave more charity than you,
we placed you at the top of our list." Then the rabbis
seated Abba Yudan among them, and they recited for
him this verse, *A person's gift makes room for the person, and brings that person before the great ones.*

This story promises what no one can deliver: a sure reward
for doing good. It is a hopeful promise. We surely want to
believe in it. In our own terms, the reward may be seen as
position and public recognition. You can be more certain of that
kind of reward than of one consisting of fields and cattle. But,
given that, this side of the tradition of tzedakah, while natural
and heartening, is to be reserved for fables. Indeed, the end of
the tale is the thing. The hero gets to sit among great sages. That
was a legitimate reward of tzedakah then; and, changing sages
into senators or Israeli generals, it is a commonplace reward of
tzedakah now. But, as we shall immediately find, there is
another view of the matter.

2. The following story was told of Rabbi Tarfon. He was
very wealthy, but gave sparingly to the poor. Once

> Rabbi Akiba met him and said, "Master, would you like
> me to purchase for you one or two towns?" Rabbi Tar-
> fon responded, "Surely!" and promptly handed four
> thousand golden *dinars* to Rabbi Akiba. He took the
> money and distributed it to some needy students. Some
> days later, Rabbi Tarfon met him and inquired, "Where
> are the towns which you have purchased for me?" Tak-
> ing him by the hand, Rabbi Akiba led him to the school
> and summoned a pupil who had the book of Psalms in
> hand. The pupil began reciting [from the book] and
> continued until he reached the verse, *That person has
> distributed freely; that person has given to the poor;
> that person's righteousness endures forever.* Rabbi
> Akiba exclaimed, "This is the town which I have pur-
> chased for you!" Rabbi Tarfon embraced him, saying,
> "My teacher, my superior—my teacher in wisdom, my
> superior in civil conduct"—and he continued to give
> Akiba riches for distribution.

The climax of the story is reached in the verse of Scripture, in
which the word tzedakah appears. If one gives money to the
poor, this act of righteousness-which-is-charity endures forever.
What Rabbi Akiba did with the money—make provision for
poor disciples—defines the promise of eternity. Rabbi Tarfon
wished to make an investment. Rabbi Akiba made the safest one.
The paradox is obvious, the point self-revealing. The lesson
Monobases taught his brothers is a parallel to this text. The
message is exactly the same, despite the fact that the two stories
are very different in tone and setting.

FOR OUR COMMUNITY

The notion of investing in deeds of tzedakah is appealing in an
age when investments often prove the path to wealth. As an
eternal people, Jews are urged to see the investment in tzedakah
as a lasting one. But we should not see these investments in
terms of philanthropy alone. Tzedakah takes many forms, then

and now. Listen to the opening passage of Mishnah, tractate Peah, which deals with one form of gifts to the poor:

> **These are things, the return on which a person enjoys in this world, and principal of which endures for the world to come: honoring one's father and mother, performing acts of loving-kindness, and bringing peace to those who quarrel; but the study of Torah is worth all of these put together.**

Tzedakah is represented in all these. The investment is in eternity.

Can Jewish Philanthropy Buy Jewish Survival?

So far as Jews in the United States and Canada can work together at all, it is in tzedakah, interpreted broadly. Split into various movements and sects, we pray in different ways. Some will not eat what others regard as good food. Fair numbers marry contrary to the rules observed by the majority. We do not live in close quarters, in the same neighborhoods, any more. We can scarcely tell who is Jewish through names, let alone faces. In all of these ways, and in many others, we hardly constitute a community of faith, let alone an extended family joined by common heritage and shared belief. If truth be told, even the State of Israel no longer serves to unite us, except in the conviction that the Jewish state must survive. But when it comes to specific policies meant to ensure that survival, we are no more unanimous than we are on whether or not to eat shellfish. In all, how can we work together, and what can we accomplish in union with one another?

There is one solid, factual response. What unites us is our shared convictions about common responsibilities to one another here at home and throughout the world. That is demonstrated in two ways.

First of all, the Jewish Federations and welfare funds in every community do win the support of people who have, as Jews, little else in common. From assimilationist to ethnic nationalist, from Reform to Young Israel to Reconstructionist to Yeshiva-Orthodox, there is a consensus stretching from nearly one wall to the other. More important, when it comes to personal commitment, people give their time and effort to Federations—people who do not pray, do not study, do not build a *sukkah* on Sukkot, do not light candles on Friday evening or even on Hanukkah. And the same may be said of the many philanthropic organizations and institutions that represent the communal will of the Jewish people. If we are to believe the statistics, then we must conclude that the sole agency for the unification of Jews into a Jewish community, cutting across lines of fiercely held differences, is Jewish philanthropy in our various communities.

Second, if we broaden the definition of tzedakah to include all of the organizational activities of the community, then the one thing Jews actually do in common—as distinct from shared sentiments about a few important things—is write checks. That is, if you want to know what anyone is apt to do who is Jewish, in order to display loyalty and to participate in the Jewish world, it will be to join an organization, including a synagogue as one among other organizations, and to pay some money over in support of that organization. Accordingly, people who do not perceive as a Jewish deed the matter of what they eat, or the clothing they wear, or the person they or their children marry, or the books they read, will regard as a Jewish deed that simple act of making out a check to the right payee.

Now these two facts define the basis for collective Jewish existence in North America today: the conviction that the Federation or welfare fund encompasses us all, however we are divided in all other ways; the fact that the one thing we do in common as Jews is the perfectly natural secular one of transferring money from our checking accounts to a Jewish account, whatever it may be. The action in general and the shared cause in particular tell us that, as I said at the outset, all we have in common is Jewish philanthropy, tzedakah in its innumerable forms and expressions, but in the Federations above all.

It must follow that, if we view the Jews as a whole, taking seriously not only the maximalists but also the minimalists, who are more numerous, we must conclude that if Jewish philanthropy cannot buy Jewish survival, there is no other program and ideal that can. If we care about our old and our young, our stragglers as well as our pioneers, then we must recognize that the lowest common denominator—belief in Federations, the shared act of giving—also is the only common denominator among us. So far as we are Jews together, without qualifying adjectives such as Reform Jews or B'nai B'rith Jews or Zionist or Jewish Defense League or Torah-True Jews, it is a community bounded by budgets and expressed through a shared deed of donation. It further follows that, if we are to shape a way of life common to us all, a way of life to define what makes us a community at all, it will have to emerge from the world of Jewish philanthropy. So, to reiterate, if Jewish philanthropy cannot buy Jewish survival, nothing can, no one will.

Alas.

On the face of it, Jewish philanthropy demands too little from us, changes us insufficiently. That is to say, if all it takes to be a Jew is to write a check, then being a Jew is not terribly different from being a consumer of electricity or a customer at a department store. Being Jewish is a minor aspect of the existence through consumption of material things that defines happiness for us. Indeed, we transform and translate being Jewish into terms of a larger society in which, whatever you are takes the form of a transfer of something valuable, meaning, money and the things money buys. A generation earlier, Jews thought that certain kinds of food defined the joys of being Jewish, a pastrami sandwich is the highlight of a song about Jewish Roumania. Today I think belly-Judaism is a memory for most of us, with more delicate tastes than for pastrami. A while ago, we could define Jewishness in terms of engagement in the life of the renewal of Israel the Jewish people through the State of Israel. Now we know that, with upwards of 300,000 Israeli emigrants in our own community, salvation is not apt to come from the east to the soul of North American Jewry. A lift perhaps, a constant, gnawing concern surely, but not salvation: not the message of who we are and what we are supposed to be. So we are left with philanthropy, and that means writing a check.

I am aware that people think Jewish philanthropy is more than merely writing a check, because of the things money can buy through the check. Every organization accomplishes great things. Every Jewish institution, sustained by the Federations and welfare funds, serves splendid purposes. Some time back, many of us argued that the Jewish Federations spent more on nonsectarian than on distinctively Jewish causes, more on hospitals than on schools, more on teaching good things about Jews to gentiles than teaching Judaism to Jews. Times have changed for the better—though, obviously, institutions that express the Jewishness of Jews, whether Brandeis University and Dropsie College and Jewish Theological Seminary and Hebrew Union College, or synagogues and temples, or yeshivot and day schools, or youth groups and summer camps of all kinds, continue to struggle. Yet, in the main, so far as money can buy survival the Jewish community continues to improve in the level of investing in the things that make Jews Jewish. More important, the Jews in Federations themselves care about the same things that engage their critics, so that today, unlike the bad old days, there is essential agreement on both means and ends. Where there may be disagreement, it concerns only dollars and cents, in a framework of shared sensibility.

Jewish philanthropy's power to buy Jewish survival is in doubt for a different reason. The budgets, if not ideal, are at least shaped to point in the right directions. The Federations take seriously the education of their donors. Leadership training programs teach more than proper ways of approaching potential donors. What remains troubling is not the material expression of philanthropy, what the Federations and organizations do with their money. Nor is it the charge of materialism, since we all recognize that to accomplish anything in this place and age, you have to have money to buy time, that is, life.

What is disheartening is the reason that the Federations and organizations serve to unite us all. It is that they are understood as essentially neutral and fundamentally secular instrumentalities. The reason we can all agree on the importance of giving, the explanation for our willingness to work together with others who differ on all else only when it comes to raising funds for the Federation or some other good Jewish cause, is the very neutrality of the act of giving, the secular character of the act of writing a check. We can agree to write a check to the Federation, doing precisely what every other Jew does, because we understand that this simple, secular deed is both Jewish and good while at the same time unthreatening and unaffecting.

It is time to unpack this notion that we share about the neutrality of Jewish giving, its universal appeal as what we do— the only thing we do—with most other Jews most of the time. It seems fair to say that the appeal of what is called "checkbook" Judaism is that it is supposed to leave us untouched. It is the path of least resistance; it demands nothing more than our money, but no part of our soul. That attitude represents the conventional wisdom of the day: "Everybody doesn't like somebody, but nobody doesn't like Federation (or, substitute ORT, National Council of Jewish Women, and so on)." That unanimity of opinion is possible because there is nothing to dislike, because nothing is asked of us but what we have and can dispense, a few dollars for this and that. In many ways, Jewish philanthropy stands in the minds of both participants and critics as a Jewish cop-out, a way of paying a ransom for the absent soul.

If that is understood as the truth, then Jewish philanthropy cannot buy Jewish survival, because Jewish philanthropy really is not an important Jewish deed, not an expression of Jewish commitment. If, when we give money, we really think we are buying back the right to be indifferent and separate from the community, then by giving, we buy the right not to give: we give money, we keep our souls, our selves, to ourselves. In such a pattern there is no community, nothing worthy of survival. The very thing that unites us, if this view is correct, also dissolves the ties that bind us together. *If the act of writing a check is neutral because we do the same thing in a hundred different causes, then the act of writing a Jewish check is one of drawing against an empty account.*

The root of the problem is not what we do, but the way we view what we do. Seeing Jewish philanthropy as a cop-out from being Jewish is a flagrant misunderstanding of Jewish philanthropists, which is to say, of all Jews who give money to Jewish causes, thus, pretty much all of us.

First, Jewish organizations and philanthropic agencies demand much more from us than a few dollars. They need our time, to provide a constituency and leadership. They need to enlist some of us for boards. They require people to run the campaigns as volunteers. They depend upon people to fill up the chairs and to sit at meetings night after night. People active in the Jewish community are rightly sick and tired of being called checkbook Jews. They express their Jewish commitment through writing checks—which speak for them, act for them. They know that—more than their money—they give of their time, energy, and commitment.

When you pick up a phone and call a Jewish neighbor for a pledge, you put yourself on the line. Perhaps salespeople are used to this kind of relationship. The rest of us find it acutely painful, yet many of us do it. When you give up a free evening and go down to yet another meeting, sit through yet another mass of details about one thing and the other, you give more than money. You give a small piece of your life.

When you enter into the relationships of conflict and disagreement about policy, program, or planning, you take on burdens you don't need. You cannot serve on a committee without entering into points of discord and conflict, joining in the interplay between persons and personalities. All of us are private people. None of us needs the hassle. Many of us accept it. Stay home, and no one thwarts your will or shows you up. Go to meetings, and everyone does. It is in the nature of the life of people working together.

Conflict creates community. Indifference, isolation, merely writing checks—these are hardly the raw materials of the life of your community. We live because we argue with one another. We give because we care. We participate as Jews. Otherwise, we do not need all the trouble.

Second, and still more important, if it is the fact that when we give as Jews, we live as Jews, then our very basic conception of philanthropy has to be revised. People tend to think it is secular, neutral, merely good. But if philanthropy stands for a viewpoint and a commitment, there is nothing neutral or secular in Jewish giving. On the contrary, we give as the end product of prior reflection, deeper commitment. We give as an act of belief. If we did not believe, we also would not care; and if we did not care, we surely would not give.

So the act of writing a check *in context* does not differ in any important way from the act of saying a blessing *in context*, or the act of studying Torah, that is, the act of Jewish learning *in context*. If you happen to be interested in poetry and come across a poem that is a prayer in the Jewish prayer book and read that poem-prayer, that is not an act of worship. If you happen to be curious about some fact and take up a Jewish holy book to find that fact, that is not an act of study of Torah. And if you happen to write a check for some cause that passes your mind, even though it goes for a Jewish purpose, that is not an act of tzedakah, of Jewish philanthropy.

But if you read the poem intending it as a prayer, if you study the Jewish text intending it as Torah, if you write the check intending it as your statement of responsibility to the Jewish people and community—in all three instances, you do a holy deed. And one deed is not different from any other. All are equally holy since our intention, our attitude, makes them holy. The deed is neutral. We make the difference. The action may mean anything. In our heart we impose its true meaning.

What is in our heart and in our mind, therefore, decides whether something is ordinary or holy. It is not the act of writing the check. It is our attitude, our *kavanah* (Hebrew: intention), in writing the check. I want to spell this out with some care, since I believe it is the critical issue before us. Whether or not Jewish philanthropy can buy Jewish survival is a question settled in one way only: what we mean through tzedakah, through Jewish philanthropy.

The Challenge of Tzedakah

The Talmud presents the challenge that we as a Jewish community face today by means of the following passage: Doing tzedakah is the only way in which a person can *walk after the Lord your God.*

> **Rabbi Assi said, Tzedakah is as important as all the other commandments put together.**

So we must ask, In doing tzedakah, do Jews see themselves as carrying out commandments? In the skillful work of organizations and institutions of Jewry, are we doing something holy? What does holiness mean? That is the question before us.

Tzedakah is to be seen as a challenge. To those Conservative Jews who put on a kippah when they enter the synagogue but not otherwise and so want their heads covered when they pray, I ask, must one put on a kippah when he or she works for the Federation? Conservative Jews may want to wear a kippah when they walk and talk with the rabbi of their synagogue. do they have to put on a kippah in the office of the executive director or president of the Jewish Federation?

Reform Jews feel a sense of reverence and awe in the beautiful temples they have built throughout the continent. They respect and even revere their rabbis, too. Do they see the Federation office as a holy place? Should there be a sermon and choir at Federation meetings?

Orthodox Jews say a *berakhah,* a blessing, when they perform a religious deed: ". . . who has made us holy through commandments, and commanded us to. . . ." What is the blessing to say when one writes out a check to the Federation?

In asking these questions, I present the principal dilemma confronting both the so-called secular and the so-called religious Jews. It is this: When as a Jew am I secular, and when am I religious? My own view is that I am only and always a Jew. My task is to make the ordinary into something unusual, the everyday into something Jewish, to consecrate the profane, but also to sanctify God's name in this world. The Torah tells me I have to make what is holy out of something worldly, so that the world may become holy.

If you are Reform, I am not asking you to wear a head-covering when you pray. I am asking you to extend your deepest convictions about why you belong to a temple to the matter of what you do when you contribute to the Federation and work for it or for its constituent agencies. The ordinary is to be made holy—by your attitude.

If you are Orthodox, I am not asking you to regard attendance at a Federation meeting as equivalent to davening *minhah* (reciting the afternoon prayers). I am asking you to take to heart the *torah* of building the community as a principle mitzvah of our time. My notion is that the same sense of holiness attached to study of Torah must also pertain to doing the "secular" deed of making a phone call in behalf of the Federation. The commonplace is to be sanctified—by your heart.

If you are Conservative or Reconstructionist and regularly attend Shabbat morning services (and not many do), I am asking you to reflect on the equivalent importance of what you do Sunday morning or Tuesday evening in a Federation program. The wall between secular and religious must fall—in your heart.

Further Demands

There are other requirements. Let me express these as negative challenges: Do you really maintain that all you do is in the here and now? Is work for the Federation not much more than public service and a hobby? Clearly, we work for the Federation, for B'nai B'rith, for the local day school, because we want to do something positively Jewish.

Our critics say we are looking for standing, or business opportunities, or social life. But we know that if that were all we wanted, if we were merely seeking *kovod* (honor) or succumbing to social pressure, we should have fulfilled our purposes long ago and gotten out. We're still there, at our telephones, sitting in hard chairs at budget committee meetings, listening to speakers who say things we heard last year and know we'll hear next year.

It must follow that we take up the tasks of tzedakah because we believe certain things, not merely because we want certain things. If people say it is merely materialistic, we must answer that it is not so. When we work in Jewish philanthropy or in Jewish organizations because we are Jews, we express the right attitude even as we do the right thing.

Why? Stated simply, Judaism has always maintained that the Jewish people is holy. And holiness is not limited to a holy place—a temple, synagogue, or school. The holiness of Israel, the Jewish people, inheres in us as a people, as individuals. What we do contains the potentiality of being holy since we ᴜs Israel, as the Jewish people, do it. Accordingly, the faith of Judaism forms a bridge between this-worldly, practical things— raising money for Jewish purposes, working for Jewish causes— and supposedly otherworldly things, like praying or studying Torah.

How to build the bridge?

Tzedakah is Holy

All depends on what *you* think as you carry out a common deed. Your attitude changes the secular into the sacred. Such is the fundamental judgment of the Judaic religious tradition, expressed in law and theology alike, upon how we make the common into the holy, how we sanctify the secular.

The act of tzedakah by definition is holy. When you work for tzedakah, you are doing the equivalent of prayer or study or keeping the Sabbath or carrying out any other mitzvah. Not only so, but if you do nothing else but tzedakah, you are doing what is all-important.

The task before us all is to take a new view of a familiar deed. We can no longer permit ourselves, nor can we permit others, to regard it as a merely secular act. What is secular must be made sacred. And the power to make it so, the power to change your inner model of the world from a secular to a holy one, lies fully within you.

What we say in our hearts, our attitudes, and our intentions, these make the difference. If you light a candle on Thursday, it gives light. Light a candle on Friday at sunset and you do a holy deed. The act is the same. The circumstance and the attitude are not. We decide. We have the power of making things holy through our decisions and our actions. Ours is the capacity for sanctification.

Jewish law provides us with guidelines. The step from commandment to sanctification is not long. Jews are obligated to do tzedakah. It may be the one commandment some Jews acknowledge. But they do it and affirm it with all their hearts and souls. Many Jews work to keep this commandment. Quite correctly, we insist others keep it. We come to the Jewish community at large with zeal; we make demands with righteousness. We are right to be zealous. We are duty-bound to make demands.

Is this not in fact the intention needed to turn an ordinary deed into an extraordinary one? For some Jews tzedakah is the paramount duty of the Jew. Such Jews must be regarded as religious. Judaism leaves no choice.

But can the essentially secular Jew, to whom tzedakah is all, see matters this way?

A Jewish Model of the World

The logic of Judaism is that, without intending to express religious commitment, the so-called secular Jew does a deed that is fully and completely an act of piety. How so? The Jew in question does the act in exactly the spirit in which we do it if we are pious: with commitment and with concern.

What must follow is this: a sense of purpose. The deed, well done, must be done to express a sacred ideal.

Now, if you ask Jews who do tzedakah why they do it, the answer will generaly be: "To help Israel, to help other Jews." Surely these are the holiest of holy purposes.

Nothing then is lacking! (1) The deed is well done; and (2) the deed is done for a holy cause. How is it different from kindling a candle at sunset on Friday?

The mitzvah of tzedakah may be paramount, it may even serve to define Jewish life, but no mitzvah on its own can be the sum total of Jewish life. The pinnacle without the mountain does not exist. There are other deeds to be well done, for holy purposes. These too are likely to strike so-called "secular" Jews as quite familiar. Studying Torah is a religious duty. Is reading a book "studying Torah?" It is, if you intend it to be so. In our day, we may visit the State of Israel. It may be tourism or it may be pilgrimage. It all depends on us, on what is in our heart.

But that is always the issue. The whole world and everything in it belongs to God. Everything may be holy—if we make it so. When we raise our eyes and look upward, in our hearts and minds we acknowledge Heaven, creation. The stars are the same. We perceive them as works of creation, singing the glory of the Creator. Or we may not see them at all. So much depends on the model of the world we fashion for ourselves and carry within us. The issue of tzedakah captures the very soul of the Jewish problem of our day: our vision of the stars—and of ourselves.

APPENDIX

Tzedakah is based on primary sources gleaned from the *Mishneh Torah*, the law code compiled by Maimonides; the Babylonian and Jerusalem Talmuds; and other rabbinic collections. The translations that appear in the course of the narrative are faithful paraphrases of the original texts. For general purposes, such translation suffices.

But the sources themselves will reward a more intensive study. They are reprinted in this Appendix, in the original Hebrew or Aramaic, along with more technical, hence, literal translations.

Torah and Tzedakah

מַעֲשֶׂה בְּמֻנְבָּז הַמֶּלֶךְ
שֶׁעָמַד וּבִזְבֵּז אוֹצְרוֹתָיו
בִּשְׁנֵי בַצָּרוֹת.
שָׁלְחוּ לוֹ אֶחָיו,

A. Monobases the King [of Adiabene] went and gave away [to the poor all of] his treasures during years of famine.
B. His brothers sent [the following message] to him:

אֲבוֹתֶיךָ גָּנְזוּ אוֹצָרוֹת
וְהוֹסִיפוּ עַל שֶׁל אֲבוֹתָם,
וְאַתָּה עָמַדְתָּ וּבִזְבַּזְתָּ אֶת
כָּל אוֹצְרוֹתֶיךָ שֶׁלְּךָ וְשֶׁל
אֲבוֹתֶיךָ.

C. "Your ancestors stored up treasures and increased the wealth [left for them by] their ancestors. But you went and gave away all of these treasures, both your own and those of your ancestors!"

אָמַר לָהֶם, אֲבוֹתַי גָּנְזוּ
אוֹצָרוֹת לְמַטָּה, וַאֲנִי גָּנַזְתִּי
לְמַעְלָה, שֶׁנֶּאֱמַר: אֱמֶת
מֵאֶרֶץ תִּצְמָח, וְצֶדֶק
מִשָּׁמַיִם נִשְׁקָף;

D. He replied to them, "My ancestors stored up treasures for this lower [world], but I have stored up treasures for [the heavenly world] above, as it is stated [in Scripture], *Faithfulness will spring up from the ground below, and righteousness* (ṣdq) *will look down from the sky* PS. 85:12.

אֲבוֹתַי גָּנְזוּ אוֹצָרוֹת מָקוֹם
שֶׁהַיָּד שׁוֹלֶטֶת בּוֹ, וַאֲנִי
גָּנַזְתִּי מָקוֹם שֶׁאֵין הַיָּד
שׁוֹלֶטֶת בּוֹ, שֶׁנֶּאֱמַר: צֶדֶק

E. "My ancestors stored up treasures [for the material world], where the [human] hand can reach, but I have stored up treasures [for the non-

וּמִשְׁפָּט מְכוֹן כִּסְאֶךָ, חֶסֶד
וֶאֱמֶת יְקַדְּמוּ פָנֶיךָ;

material world] where the [human] hand cannot reach, as it is stated [in Scripture], *Righteousness* (ṣdq) *and justice are the foundation of Your throne, steadfast love and faithfulness go before You* PS. 89:15.

אֲבוֹתַי גָּנְזוּ אוֹצָרוֹת שֶׁאֵין
עוֹשִׂין פֵּירוֹת, וַאֲנִי גָּנַזְתִּי
אוֹצָרוֹת שֶׁעוֹשִׂין פֵּירוֹת,
שֶׁנֶּאֱמַר: אִמְרוּ צַדִּיק כִּי
טוֹב, כִּי פְרִי מַעַלְלֵיהֶם
יֹאכֵלוּ;

F. "My ancestors stored up treasures [of a type] that produce no [real] benefits, but I have stored up treasures [of the sort] that do produce benefits, as it is stated [in Scripture], *Tell the righteous* (ṣdyq) *that it shall be well with him, for they shall reap the benefits of their deeds* ISA. 3:10.

אֲבוֹתַי גָּנְזוּ אוֹצָרוֹת מָמוֹן,
וַאֲנִי גָּנַזְתִּי אוֹצָרוֹת שֶׁל
נְפָשׁוֹת, שֶׁנֶּאֱמַר: פְּרִי צַדִּיק
עֵץ חַיִּים, וְלוֹקֵחַ נְפָשׁוֹת
חָכָם.

G. "My ancestors stored up treasures of money, but I have stored up treasures of souls, as it is stated [in Scripture], *The fruit of the righteous* (ṣdyq) *is a tree of life, and a wise man saves the souls* [of poor people] PROV. 11:30.

אֲבוֹתַי גָּנְזוּ אוֹצָרוֹת
לַאֲחֵרִים, וַאֲנִי גָּנַזְתִּי
לְעַצְמִי, שֶׁנֶּאֱמַר: וּלְךָ
תִּהְיֶה צְדָקָה לִפְנֵי ה'
אֱלֹהֶיךָ.

H. "My ancestors stored up treasures [that eventually after their deaths, would benefit only] others, but I have stored up treasures [that will benefit] myself [both in life and in death], as it is stated [in Scripture], *It shall be a righteousness* (ṣdqh) *to you before the Lord your God* DEUT. 24:13.

אֲבוֹתַי גָּנְזוּ אוֹצָרוֹת בָּעוֹלָם
הַזֶּה, וַאֲנִי גָּנַזְתִּי לְעַצְמִי
לָעוֹלָם הַבָּא, שֶׁנֶּאֱמַר,
וְהָלַךְ לְפָנֶיךָ צִדְקֶךָ.

I. "My ancestors stored up treasures in this world, but I have stored up treasures for myself in the world-to-come, as it is stated [in Scripture], *Your righteousness* (ṣdqh) *shall go before you,* [*and the glory of the Lord shall be your rear guard*] ISA. 58:8.

Laws Concerning Degrees of Tzedakah

From the Mishneh Torah:

10:7–15

שְׁמֹנֶה מַעֲלוֹת יֵשׁ בַּצְּדָקָה,
זוֹ לְמַעֲלָה מִזּוֹ: מַעֲלָה
גְדוֹלָה שֶׁאֵין לְמַעֲלָה
מִמֶּנָּה – זֶה הַמַּחֲזִיק בְּיַד
יִשְׂרָאֵל שֶׁמָּךְ וְנוֹתֵן לוֹ
מַתָּנָה אוֹ הַלְוָאָה, אוֹ
עוֹשֶׂה עִמּוֹ שֻׁתָּפוּת, אוֹ
מַמְצִיא לוֹ מְלָאכָה כְּדֵי
לְחַזֵּק אֶת־יָדוֹ עַד שֶׁלֹּא
יִצְטָרֵךְ לַבְּרִיּוֹת לִשְׁאֹל, וְעַל
זֶה נֶאֱמַר: וְהֶחֱזַקְתָּ בּוֹ גֵּר
וְתוֹשָׁב וָחַי עִמָּךְ, כְּלוֹמַר:
הַחֲזֵק בּוֹ עַד שֶׁלֹּא יִפּוֹל
וְיִצְטָרֵךְ.

A. There are eight levels of charity (ṣdqh), each one superior to the other. The highest level of all is one who supports an Israelite reduced to poverty by handing [the poor] a gift or loan, or entering into a partnership with [the poor], or finding work for [the poor], in order to support [the poor], so that [the recipient] would have no need to beg from other people. Concerning such a person [who helps the poor] it is stated [in Scripture], *You shall uphold that one; as a stranger and a settler shall* [*that person*] *live with you* LEV. 25:35, meaning support [that one], so that [that one] would not become needy.

B. Below this is the person who gives charity (ṣdqh) to the poor in such a way that [the donor] does not know to whom [the donor] has given, nor does the poor know from whom [the poor] has received. This constitutes the fulfilling of a religious duty for its own sake, and for this purpose there was a Chamber of Secrets in the Temple, to which the righteous (ṣdqym) would contribute secretly, and from which the poor of good families would draw their sustenance in equal secrecy. Almost as high is the level of [the donor] who contributes directly to the alms (ṣdqh) fund. (One should not, however, contribute directly to the alms (ṣdqh) fund unless [one] knows that the person in charge of it is trustworthy, is a sage, and knows how to manage it properly, as was the case of Rabbi Hananiah ben Teradyon.)

C. Below this is [the donor] who knows to whom [the donor] is giving, while the poor person does not know from whom [the poor person] is receiving. [The donor] is thus like the great among the Sages who used to set out secretly and throw money down at the doors of the poor. This is a proper way [of giving charity], and a preferable

פָּחוּת מִזֶּה — הַנּוֹתֵן
צְדָקָה לָעֲנִיִּים וְלֹא יָדַע לְמִי
נָתַן וְלֹא יָדַע הֶעָנִי מִמִּי
לָקַח; שֶׁהֲרֵי זוֹ מִצְוָה
לִשְׁמָהּ, כְּגוֹן לִשְׁכַּת
חֲשָׁאִים שֶׁהָיְתָה בַּמִּקְדָּשׁ
שֶׁהָיוּ הַצַּדִּיקִים נוֹתְנִין בָּהּ
בַּחֲשַׁאי וְהָעֲנִיִּים בְּנֵי טוֹבִים
מִתְפַּרְנְסִין מִמֶּנָּה בַּחֲשַׁאי.
וְקָרוֹב לָזֶה — הַנּוֹתֵן לְתוֹךְ
קֻפָּה שֶׁל צְדָקָה, וְלֹא יִתֵּן
אָדָם לְתוֹךְ קֻפָּה שֶׁל צְדָקָה
אֶלָּא־אִם־כֵּן יוֹדֵעַ
שֶׁהַמְמֻנֶּה נֶאֱמָן וְחָכָם
וְיוֹדֵעַ לְהַנְהִיג כַּשּׁוּרָה,
כְּרַבִּי חֲנַנְיָה בֶּן־תְּרַדְיוֹן.

פָּחוּת מִזֶּה — שֶׁיֵּדַע הַנּוֹתֵן
לְמִי יִתֵּן וְלֹא יָדַע הֶעָנִי
מִמִּי לָקַח, כְּגוֹן גְּדוֹלֵי
הַחֲכָמִים שֶׁהָיוּ הוֹלְכִין
בְּסֵתֶר וּמַשְׁלִיכִין הַמָּעוֹת
בְּפִתְחֵי הָעֲנִיִּים. וְכָזֶה רָאוּי
לַעֲשׂוֹת, וּמַעֲלָה טוֹבָה
הִיא, אִם אֵין הַמְמֻנִּין
בִּצְדָקָה נוֹהֲגִין כַּשּׁוּרָה.

one if those in charge of distributing alms (ṣdqh) are not conducting themselves as they should.

D. Below this is the case where the poor person knows from whom [the poor] is receiving, but the recipient remains anonymous. [The donor] who gives [charity] in this way is like those great Sages who used to place their charity in the fold of a linen sheet which they would throw over their shoulder, so that the poor who came behind them to take money were not exposed to humiliation.

E. Below this is [the donor] who hands [charity] to the poor person before being asked.

F. Below this is [the donor] who hands [charity] to the poor person after the latter has asked for it.

G. Below this is [the donor] who gives the poor person less than what is proper, but in a friendly manner.

H. Below this is [the donor] who gives [charity] with a scowl.

I. The greatest among the sages used to hand a penny to a poor person before praying, and then proceed to pray, as it is stated [in Scripture], *As for me, I shall behold Your face in righteousness* (ṣdq) PS. 17:15.

פָּחוּת מִזֶּה — שֶׁיֵּדַע הֶעָנִי מִמִּי נָטַל וְלֹא יָדַע הַנּוֹתֵן, כְּגוֹן גְּדוֹלֵי הַחֲכָמִים שֶׁהָיוּ צוֹרְרִים הַמָּעוֹת בִּסְדִינֵיהֶם וּמַפְשִׁילִין לַאֲחוֹרֵיהֶם וּבָאִין הָעֲנִיִּים וְנוֹטְלִין, כְּדֵי שֶׁלֹּא יִהְיֶה לָהֶם בּוּשָׁה.

פָּחוּת מִזֶּה — שֶׁיִּתֵּן לוֹ בְּיָדוֹ קֹדֶם שֶׁיִּשְׁאַל.

פָּחוּת מִזֶּה — שֶׁיִּתֵּן לוֹ אַחַר שֶׁיִּשְׁאַל.

פָּחוּת מִזֶּה — שֶׁיִּתֵּן לוֹ פָּחוּת מִן־הָרָאוּי בְּסֵבֶר פָּנִים יָפוֹת.

פָּחוּת מִזֶּה — שֶׁיִּתֵּן לוֹ בְּעֶצֶב.

גְּדוֹלֵי הַחֲכָמִים הָיוּ נוֹתְנִין פְּרוּטָה לֶעָנִי קֹדֶם כָּל־ תְּפִלָּה וְאַחַר כָּךְ מִתְפַּלְּלִין, שֶׁנֶּאֱמַר: אֲנִי בְּצֶדֶק אֶחֱזֶה פָנֶיךָ.

Laws Concerning Distribution of Tzedakah

1. What Do the Poor Have to Do for Themselves?

From the Mishneh Torah: 9:16

מִי שֶׁהָיוּ לוֹ בָתִּים, שָׂדוֹת
וּכְרָמִים, וְאִם מוֹכְרָם בִּימֵי
הַגְּשָׁמִים מוֹכְרָם בְּזוֹל, וְאִם
הִנִּיחָם עַד יְמוֹת הַחַמָּה
מוֹכְרָם בְּשָׁוְיֵהֶם — אֵין
מְחַיְּבִין אוֹתוֹ לִמְכֹּר, אֶלָּא
מַאֲכִילִין אוֹתוֹ מַעְשַׂר עָנִי
עַד חֲצִי דְמֵיהֶן, וְלֹא יִדְחֹק
עַצְמוֹ וְיִמְכֹּר שֶׁלֹּא בִזְמַן
מְכִירָה.

A person who owns houses, fields, and vineyards, which, if sold during the rainy season would fetch a low price, but if held back until the summer would fetch a better price, should not be made to sell them; rather, [the person] should receive out of the proceeds of the poor person's tithe up to half the value of the properties, so that person should not feel forced to sell at the wrong time.

2. What Does the Community Have to Do for the Poor?

From the Mishneh Torah: 8:3

לְפִי מַה־שֶּׁחָסֵר הֶעָנִי אַתָּה
מְצֻוֶּה לִתֵּן לוֹ: אִם אֵין לוֹ
כְּסוּת — מְכַסִּים אוֹתוֹ;
אִם אֵין לוֹ כְּלֵי בַיִת —
קוֹנִין לוֹ; אִם אֵין לוֹ
אִשָּׁה — מַשִּׂיאִין אוֹתוֹ;
וְאִם הָיְתָה אִשָּׁה מַשִּׂיאִין
אוֹתָה לְאִישׁ. אֲפִלּוּ הָיָה
דַּרְכּוֹ שֶׁל זֶה הֶעָנִי לִרְכֹּב
עַל הַסּוּס וְעֶבֶד רָץ לְפָנָיו

You are commanded to give the poor person according to [the poor person's] needs. If [the poor] has no clothing, [the poor] should be clothed. If [the poor] has no household furnishing, these should be bought for [the poor]. If the [poor] man has no wife, he should be helped to marry. If [the poor person] is a woman, she should be given in marriage. Even if [the poor

וְהֶעֱנִי וְיָרַד מִנְּכָסָיו —
קוֹנִין לוֹ סוּס לִרְכּוֹב עָלָיו
וְעֶבֶד לָרוּץ לְפָנָיו, שֶׁנֶּאֱמַר:
דֵּי מַחְסֹרוֹ אֲשֶׁר יֶחְסַר לוֹ.
וּמְצֻוֶּה אַתָּה לְהַשְׁלִים
חֶסְרוֹנוֹ וְאֵין אַתָּה מְצֻוֶּה
לְעַשְּׂרוֹ.

person] had been accustomed to ride a horse, with a servant running before, and [that person] has now become poor and lost [these] possessions, one must buy [that person] a horse to ride and a servant to run before, as it is stated [in Scripture], *Sufficient for [that person's] need in that which [the person] wants* DEUT. 15:8. You are thus obligated to support [the person's] needs; you are not, however, obligated to make [the person] wealthy.

3. How Do You Know the Poor Person Really Is Poor?

From the Mishneh Torah: 6:6

עָנִי שֶׁאֵין מַכִּירִין אוֹתוֹ
וְאָמַר: רָעֵב אֲנִי,
הַאֲכִילוּנִי — אֵין בּוֹדְקִין
אַחֲרָיו שֶׁמָּא רַמַּאי הוּא,
אֶלָּא מְפַרְנְסִין אוֹתוֹ מִיָּד.
הָיָה עָרוֹם וְאָמַר: כַּסּוּנִי —
בּוֹדְקִין אַחֲרָיו שֶׁמָּא רַמַּאי
הוּא; וְאִם הָיוּ מַכִּירִין
אוֹתוֹ — מְכַסִּין אוֹתוֹ לְפִי
כְּבוֹדוֹ מִיָּד וְאֵין בּוֹדְקִין
אַחֲרָיו.

If a poor stranger comes forth and says, "I am hungry; give me something to eat," [the stranger] should not be held suspect—[the stranger] should be fed immediately. If, however, [the stranger] has no clothing and says, "Clothe me"—[the stranger's] identity should be questioned. If [the person coming forward] is known, [that person] should be clothed immediately and appropriately, without any further inquiry.

From the Mishneh Torah: 7:13   ## 4. Who Comes First?

עָנִי שֶׁהוּא קְרוֹבוֹ — קֹדֶם
לְכָל־אָדָם; עֲנִיֵּי בֵיתוֹ —
קוֹדְמִין לַעֲנִיֵּי עִירוֹ; עֲנִיֵּי
עִירוֹ — קוֹדְמִין לַעֲנִיֵּי עִיר
אַחֶרֶת, שֶׁנֶּאֱמַר: לְאָחִיךָ,
לַעֲנִיֶּךָ וּלְאֶבְיֹנְךָ בְּאַרְצֶךָ.

A poor person who is your relative should receive your charity before all others; and [likewise] the poor of your own household have priority over the poor of your city; and the poor of your city have priority over the poor of another city, as it is stated [in Scripture], *To your poor and needy brother, in your land* DEUT. 15:11.

From the Mishneh Torah: 7:7   ## 5. Helping Gentiles Too

מְפַרְנְסִין וּמְכַסִּין עֲנִיֵּי גוֹיִם
עִם עֲנִיֵּי יִשְׂרָאֵל, מִפְּנֵי
דַּרְכֵי שָׁלוֹם. וְעָנִי הַמְחַזֵּר
עַל הַפְּתָחִים — אֵין נִזְקָקִין
לוֹ לְמַתָּנָה מְרֻבָּה, אֲבָל
נוֹתְנִין לוֹ מַתָּנָה מְעֶטֶת.
וְאָסוּר לְהַחֲזִיר אֶת־הֶעָנִי
שֶׁשָּׁאַל — רֵיקָם; וַאֲפִלּוּ
אַתָּה נוֹתֵן לוֹ גְרוֹגֶרֶת
אַחַת, שֶׁנֶּאֱמַר: אַל יָשֹׁב דַּךְ
נִכְלָם.

One must feed and clothe the heathen poor together with the Israelite poor, for the sake of peace. As for a poor person who goes from door to door, one is not obligated to give [the beggar] a large gift, but only a small one. It is forbidden to let a poor person who asks [for alms] go empty-handed; although you might give [the beggar] only one dry fig, as it is stated [in Scripture], *O let not the oppressed turn back in confusion.* PS. 74:21.

From the Mishneh Torah: 7:5

6. The Giving Is What Matters

בָּא הֶעָנִי וְשָׁאַל דֵּי מַחְסוֹרוֹ
וְאֵין יַד הַנּוֹתֵן מַשֶּׂגֶת —
נוֹתְנִין לוֹ כְּפִי הַשָּׂגַת יָדוֹ.
וְכַמָּה? עַד חֲמִשִׁית
נְכָסָיו — מִצְוָה מִן־
הַמֻּבְחָר; וְאֶחָד מֵעֲשָׂרָה
בִּנְכָסָיו — בֵּינוֹנִי; פָּחוֹת
מִכָּאן — עַיִן רָעָה.
וּלְעוֹלָם לֹא יִמְנַע עַצְמוֹ
מִשְּׁלִישִׁית הַשֶּׁקֶל בְּשָׁנָה,
וְכָל־הַנּוֹתֵן פָּחוֹת מִזֶּה לֹא
קִיֵּם מִצְוָה. וַאֲפִלּוּ עָנִי
הַמִּתְפַּרְנֵס מִן־הַצְּדָקָה —
חַיָּב לִתֵּן צְדָקָה לְאַחֵר.

If the poor person comes forth and asks for enough to satisfy [the poor person's] want from one who cannot satisfy it, the latter may give [to the poor one] as much as [the giver] can afford. How much is that? Ideally, up to one-fifth of [the donor's] possessions; up to one-tenth of [the donor's] possessions is adequate; less than this brands [the donor] as a stingy person. At no time should one permit oneself to give less than one-third of a *shekel* per year. One who gives less has not fulfilled the commandment [of tzedakah] at all. Even a poor person who lives entirely on charity (ṣdqh) must also give charity (ṣdqh) to another [poor person].

Laws Concerning Collection of Tzedakah

From the Mishneh Torah:

9:1–3

כָּל־עִיר שֶׁיֵּשׁ בָּהּ
יִשְׂרָאֵל — חַיָּבִין לְהַעֲמִיד
מֵהֶם גַּבָּאֵי צְדָקָה, אֲנָשִׁים
יְדוּעִים וְנֶאֱמָנִים שֶׁיִּהְיוּ
מְחַזְּרִין עַל הָעָם מֵעֶרֶב
שַׁבָּת לְעֶרֶב שַׁבָּת, לוֹקְחִין
מִכָּל־אֶחָד וְאֶחָד מַה שֶׁהוּא
רָאוּי לִתֵּן וְדָבָר הַקָּצוּב
עָלָיו, וְהֵם מְחַלְּקִין הַמָּעוֹת
מֵעֶרֶב שַׁבָּת לְעֶרֶב שַׁבָּת,
וְנוֹתְנִין לְכָל־עָנִי וְעָנִי
מְזוֹנוֹת הַמַּסְפִּיקִין לְשִׁבְעָה
יָמִים — וְזוֹ הִיא הַנִּקְרָא:
קֻפָּה.
פַּת וּמִינֵי מַאֲכָל אוֹ פֵּרוֹת
אוֹ מָעוֹת מִמִּי שֶׁמִּתְנַדֵּב
לְפִי שָׁעָה, וּמְחַלְּקִין אֶת־
הַגָּבוּי לָעֶרֶב בֵּין הָעֲנִיִּים
וְנוֹתְנִין לְכָל־עָנִי מִמֶּנּוּ
פַּרְנָסַת יוֹמוֹ — וְזֶהוּ
הַנִּקְרָא: תַּמְחוּי.

1. Collecting Tzedakah

A. In every city where Israelites reside, the inhabitants must appoint from among themselves well-known and trustworthy persons to act as charity (ṣdqh) collectors, who collect from the people every Friday. [The collectors] should demand from each person what is proper for [that person] to give or what [that person] has been assessed for; and should distribute the money every Friday, giving each poor person enough [charity] for seven days. This is what is called "the alms fund."

B. They must also appoint other collectors to gather every day, from each courtyard, bread and other edibles, fruits, or money from anyone who is willing to make a voluntary offering. They should distribute these that same evening among the poor, giving to each poor person [that person's] sustenance for the day. This is what is called "the charity tray."

מֵעוֹלָם לֹא רָאִינוּ וְלֹא
שָׁמַעְנוּ בְּקָהָל מִיִּשְׂרָאֵל
שֶׁאֵין לָהֶם קֻפָּה שֶׁל
צְדָקָה; אֲבָל תַּמְחוּי — יֵשׁ
מְקוֹמוֹת שֶׁנָּהֲגוּ בּוֹ וְיֵשׁ
מְקוֹמוֹת שֶׁלֹּא נָהֲגוּ בּוֹ.
וְהַמִּנְהָג הַפָּשׁוּט הַיּוֹם:
שֶׁיִּהְיוּ גַּבָּאֵי הַקֻּפָּה מְחַזְּרִין
בְּכָל־יוֹם, וּמְחַלְּקִין מֵעֶרֶב
שַׁבָּת לְעֶרֶב שַׁבָּת.

C. We have never seen nor heard of an Israelite community that does not have an alms fund. As for a charity tray, there are some places where it is customary to have it, and some where it is not. Nowadays, the general custom is for the collectors of the alms fund to go around every day, and to distribute the proceeds every Friday [preceding Shabbat].

From the Babylonian Talmud:

Taanit 21b

לֹא מְקוֹמוֹ שֶׁל אָדָם
מְכַבְּדוֹ, אֶלָּא אָדָם מְכַבֵּד
אֶת מְקוֹמוֹ.

It is not the position that honors the person, but the person that honors the position.

From the Mishneh Torah: 9:5

2. Who Collects Tzedakah?

הַקֻּפָּה אֵינָה נִגְבֵּית אֶלָּא
בִּשְׁנַיִם, שֶׁאֵין עוֹשִׂים
שְׂרָרָה עַל הַצִּבּוּר בְּמָמוֹן
בְּפָחוֹת מִשְּׁנַיִם. וּמֻתָּר
לְהַאֲמִין לְאֶחָד, הַמָּעוֹת
שֶׁל קֻפָּה. וְאֵינָה נֶחְלֶקֶת

Contributions to the alms fund must be collected jointly by two persons, because a demand for money may not be presented to the community by less than two [collectors]. Although the money collected may be entrusted [for

אֶלָּא בִּשְׁלֹשָׁה, מִפְּנֵי שֶׁהִיא
כְּדִינֵי מָמוֹנוֹת: שֶׁנּוֹתְנִים
לְכָל־אֶחָד דֵּי מַחְסוֹרוֹ
לְשַׁבָּת; וְהַתַּמְחוּי נִגְבֶּה
בִּשְׁלֹשָׁה, שֶׁאֵינוֹ דָּבָר קָצוּב,
וּמִתְחַלֵּק בִּשְׁלֹשָׁה.

safekeeping] to one person, it must be distributed by three persons because it is similar to money involved in a civil action, since they must give to each [poor person] enough for [the poor person's] weekly needs. [Donations to] the charity tray must be collected by three persons since the contribution to it is not fixed, and must [also] be distributed by three [persons].

From the Mishneh Torah: 7:10

מִי שֶׁאֵינוֹ רוֹצֶה לִתֵּן
צְדָקָה, אוֹ שֶׁיִּתֵּן מְעַט מִמַּה
שֶּׁרָאוּי לוֹ — בֵּית דִּין
כּוֹפִין אוֹתוֹ וּמַכִּין אוֹתוֹ
מַכַּת מַרְדּוּת עַד שֶׁיִּתֵּן מַה
שֶּׁאֲמָדוּהוּ לִתֵּן, וְיוֹרְדִין
לִנְכָסָיו בְּפָנָיו וְלוֹקְחִין מִמֶּנּוּ
מַה שֶּׁרָאוּי לוֹ לִתֵּן.
וּמְמַשְׁכְּנִין עַל הַצְּדָקָה,
וַאֲפִלּוּ בְּעַרְבֵי שַׁבָּתוֹת.

3. How to Deal with Refusal

The one who refuses to give charity (ṣdqh), or gives less than [that person] can afford, must be compelled by the court to give an appropriate sum, and must be flogged for disobedience until [that person] gives as much as the court estimates is proper. The court may even seize [that person's] property in [that person's] presence and take from [the person] what is proper for [that person] to give. One may pawn [possessions] in order to give charity (ṣdqh), even on the eve of the Sabbath.

4. How to Deal with Excessive Generosity

From the Mishneh Torah: 7:11

אָדָם שׁוֹעַ שֶׁהוּא נוֹתֵן
צְדָקָה יוֹתֵר מִן־הָרָאוּי לוֹ,
אוֹ שֶׁמֵּצֵר לְעַצְמוֹ וְנוֹתֵן
לַגַּבָּאִים כְּדֵי שֶׁלֹּא
יִתְבַּיֵּשׁ — אָסוּר לְתָבְעוֹ
וְלִגְבּוֹת מִמֶּנּוּ צְדָקָה; וְגַבַּאי
שֶׁמַּכְלִימוֹ וְשׁוֹאֵל מִמֶּנּוּ —
עָתִיד לְהִפָּרַע מִמֶּנּוּ,
שֶׁנֶּאֱמַר: וּפָקַדְתִּי עַל כָּל
לֹחֲצָיו.

A generous person who gives charity (ṣdqh) beyond what [that person] can afford, or denies self in order to give to the collector [of alms] so that [that person] would not be embarrassed, should not be asked to contribute charity (ṣdqh). Any alms collector who humiliates [such a person] by demanding [charity] from [that person] will surely be called to account for it, as it is stated [in Scripture], *I will punish all that oppress them* JER. 30:20.

5. The Status of a Pledge

From the Mishneh Torah: 8:1

הַצְּדָקָה הֲרֵי הִיא בִּכְלַל
הַנְּדָרִים. לְפִיכָךְ הָאוֹמֵר:
הֲרֵי עָלַי סֶלַע לִצְדָקָה, אוֹ
הֲרֵי הַסֶּלַע זוֹ צְדָקָה —
חַיָּב לִתְּנָהּ לָעֲנִיִּים מִיָּד;
וְאִם אֵחַר — עָבַר בְּבַל
תְּאַחֵר, שֶׁהֲרֵי בְיָדוֹ לִתֵּן
מִיָּד וַעֲנִיִּים מְצוּיִּין הֵם. אֵין
שָׁם עֲנִיִּים, מַפְרִישׁ וּמַנִּיחַ
עַד שֶׁיִּמְצָא עֲנִיִּים. וְאִם

Charity (ṣdqh) is subject to the rules governing vows. Therefore one who says, "I obligate myself to give a *sela* to charity," or "This *sela* is for charity," is obligated to give it to the poor immediately. If [that donor] delays, [the donor] violates the commandment, *You shall not be slack to pay it* DEUT. 23:22; if it is within [the donor's] power to dispense the *sela* immediately, and there are many poor people to be found. If there are no poor nearby, [the donor] may set aside the *sela* until poor people are located. If [the donor] stipulates that [the donor] shall give only when a poor person is found, [the donor] need not set aside the amount of the pledge. Similarly, if [the donor] stipulates when [the donor] makes a vow or a voluntary offering to charity (ṣdqh) that the alms collectors are to be free to change his *sela* or to combine it with others for conversion into gold coin, they are permitted to do so.

הִתְנָה שֶׁלֹא יִתֵּן עַד שֶׁיִּמָּצֵא עָנִי — אֵינוֹ צָרִיךְ לְהַפְרִישׁ. וְכֵן אִם הִתְנָה בְּשָׁעָה שֶׁנָּדַר בִּצְדָקָה אוֹ הִתְנַדֵּב אוֹתָהּ, שֶׁיִּהְיוּ הַגַּבָּאִין רַשָּׁאִין לְשַׁנּוֹתָהּ וּלְצָרְפָהּ בְּזָהָב — הֲרֵי אֵלּוּ מֻתָּרִין.

6. Schnorring

From the Mishneh Torah: 10:6

As for the one who presses others to give charity (ṣdqh) and persuades them to do so, [that person's] reward is greater than the reward of one who gives [charity], as it is stated [in Scripture], *And the work of righteousness* (ṣdqh) *shall be peace* ISA. 32:17.

הַכּוֹפֶה אֲחֵרִים לִתֵּן צְדָקָה וּמְעַשֶׂה אוֹתָם, שְׂכָרוֹ גָּדוֹל מִשְּׂכַר הַנּוֹתֵן, שֶׁנֶּאֱמַר: וְהָיָה מַעֲשֵׂה הַצְּדָקָה שָׁלוֹם.

From the Ordinary to the Holy

Tzedakah and Holiness

אָמַר רַבִּי חַמָּא בְּרַבִּי
חֲנִינָא, מַהוּ שֶׁנֶּאֱמַר: אַחֲרֵי
ה' אֱלֹהֵיכֶם תֵּלֵכוּ — וְכִי
אֶפְשָׁר לוֹ לְאָדָם לַהֲלֹךְ
אַחַר הַשְּׁכִינָה? וַהֲלֹא כְּבָר
נֶאֱמַר: כִּי ה' אֱלֹהֶיךָ אֵשׁ
אֹכְלָה הוּא? אֶלָּא הַלֵּךְ
אַחַר מִדּוֹתָיו שֶׁל הַקָּדוֹשׁ־
בָּרוּךְ־הוּא. מַה הוּא
הִלְבִּישׁ עֲרֻמִּים, שֶׁנֶּאֱמַר:
וַיַּעַשׂ ה' אֱלֹהִים לְאָדָם
וּלְאִשְׁתּוֹ כָּתְנוֹת עוֹר
וַיַּלְבִּשֵׁם — אַף אַתָּה
הַלְבֵּשׁ עֲרֻמִּים; הַקָּדוֹשׁ
בָּרוּךְ הוּא בִּקֵּר חוֹלִים,
שֶׁנֶּאֱמַר: וַיֵּרָא אֵלָיו
ה' בְּאֵלֹנֵי מַמְרֵא — אַף
אַתָּה בַּקֵּר חוֹלִים; הַקָּדוֹשׁ־
בָּרוּךְ־הוּא קָבַר מֵתִים,
שֶׁנֶּאֱמַר: וַיִּקְבֹּר אֹתוֹ
בַּגַּי — אַף אַתָּה קְבֹר
מֵתִים; הַקָּדוֹשׁ־בָּרוּךְ־הוּא
נִחַם אֲבֵלִים, שֶׁנֶּאֱמַר: וַיְהִי
אַחֲרֵי מוֹת אַבְרָהָם וַיְבָרֶךְ

Said Rabbi Hama, son of Rabbi Hanina, What is the meaning [of the verse]: *You shall walk behind the Lord your God* DEUT. 13:5? [Could this verse mean that] a person may [actually] walk behind the Divine Presence? [Surely not! For] is it not also stated [in Scripture], *for the Lord your God is a devouring fire* DEUT. 4:24? Rather, [the former verse must mean that] a person should imitate the [righteous] ways of the Holy One, the Blessed. Just as the Lord clothed the naked—as it is stated [in Scripture], *And the Lord God made for Adam and for his wife coats of skin, and clothed them* GEN. 3:21—so, too, you must supply clothes for the naked poor. Just as the Holy One, the Blessed, visited the sick—as it is stated [in Scripture], *And the Lord appeared [to Abraham who was recuperating] by the oaks of Mamre* GEN. 18:1—so, too, you should visit the sick. Just as the Holy One, the Blessed, buried the

אֱלֹהִים אֶת־יִצְחָק בְּנוֹ —
אַף אַתָּה נַחֵם אֲבֵלִים.

dead—as it is stated [in Scripture], *And the Lord buried [Moses] in the valley* DEUT. 34:6—so, too, you must bury the dead. Just as the Holy One, the Blessed, comforted mourners—as it is stated [in Scripture], *And it came to be after the death of Abraham that God blessed Isaac his son* GEN. 25:11—so, too, you should comfort mourners.

From the Tanhuma:

Leviticus 17a

אֲנִי בְּצֶדֶק אֶחֱזֶה פָנֶיךָ —
בּוֹא וּרְאֵה כַּמָּה גָדוֹל כֹּחָהּ
שֶׁל צְדָקָה, שֶׁבִּשְׁבִיל
פְּרוּטָה אַחַת שֶׁאָדָם נוֹתֵן
לְעָנִי זוֹכֶה וּמְקַבֵּל פְּנֵי
שְׁכִינָה. בְּנֹהַג שֶׁבָּעוֹלָם
מַטְרוֹנָה שֶׁהִיא מְבַקֶּשֶׁת
לִרְאוֹת אֶת־הַמֶּלֶךְ
וּלְהַקְבִּיל פָּנָיו הִיא עוֹשָׂה
עֲטָרָה לְפִי כְבוֹדָהּ, וְעַל־יְדֵי
עֲטָרָה שֶׁמַּכְנֶסֶת לְעַטֵּר
אֶת־הַמֶּלֶךְ הִיא רוֹאָה פְּנֵי
הַמֶּלֶךְ, וּבִפְרוּטָה שֶׁאָדָם
נוֹתֵן לְעָנִי זוֹכֶה וּמְקַבֵּל פְּנֵי
שְׁכִינָה.

A. *Through the righteousness-of-charity* (ṣdq), *I shall behold Your face* PS. 17:15. Notice that [this verse illustrates the] immense power of charity (ṣdqh): For [the verse indicates that] a person who gives [as little as] a single penny to the poor is deemed worthy to behold the face of the Divine Presence. In the material world, [however,] it is customary that a matron who wishes to be received by her king must fashion a suitable crown [as a present for him]. And by presenting this crown, which she brings to adorn him, [the matron becomes worthy of] beholding the face of the king. But a person needs to give only a single penny to the poor in order to behold the face of the Divine Presence.

דָּבָר אַחֵר: מָה רָאָה דָוִד לְפָרֵשׁ כֹּחָהּ שֶׁל צְדָקָה בִּלְבָד? אֶלָּא לְלַמֶּדְךָ, שֶׁאֲפִלּוּ רְשָׁעִים שֶׁאֵין בְּיָדָם אֶלָּא זְכוּת שֶׁל צְדָקָה בִּלְבָד, זוֹכִים בָּהּ וּמְקַבְּלִים פְּנֵי שְׁכִינָה.

B. Furthermore, why did David [the author of Psalm 17], see fit to discuss the power of charity (ṣdqh) exclusively? [He did so deliberately] so as to demonstrate that even the wicked, who have no virtues other than the giving of charity (ṣdqh), are [nonetheless] deemed worthy to behold the face of the Divine Presence.

From the Babylonian Talmud:

Baba Batra 10a

דָּרַשׁ רַבִּי דוֹסְתַּאי בְּרַבִּי יַנַּאי: בּוֹא וּרְאֵה, שֶׁלֹּא כְּמִדַּת הַקָּדוֹשׁ-בָּרוּךְ-הוּא מִדַּת בָּשָׂר-וָדָם. מִדַּת בָּשָׂר-וָדָם, אָדָם מֵבִיא דוֹרוֹן גָּדוֹל לַמֶּלֶךְ, סָפֵק מְקַבְּלִים אוֹתוֹ הֵימֶנּוּ סָפֵק אֵין מְקַבְּלִים אוֹתוֹ הֵימֶנּוּ, וְאִם תִּמְצָא לוֹמַר: מְקַבְּלִים אוֹתוֹ הֵימֶנּוּ — סָפֵק רוֹאֶה פְּנֵי הַמֶּלֶךְ סָפֵק אֵינוֹ רוֹאֶה פְּנֵי הַמֶּלֶךְ, וְהַקָּדוֹשׁ-בָּרוּךְ-הוּא אֵינוֹ כֵן, אָדָם נוֹתֵן פְּרוּטָה לֶעָנִי

A. Rabbi Dostai, son of Rabbi Yannai, preached [the following]: Notice that the ways of flesh and blood are unlike the ways of God. The ways of [creatures of] flesh and blood are as follows. [If] a person offers an expensive present to a king, it may be accepted or it may not. Furthermore, even if the present is accepted [by the king], it is still uncertain whether the donor will be deemed worthy of an audience [with the king]. But the [ways of] the Holy One, the Blessed, [are entirely] different. A person who gives [as little as] a

זוֹכֶה וּמְקַבֵּל פְּנֵי שְׁכִינָה,
שֶׁנֶּאֱמַר: אֲנִי בְּצֶדֶק אֶחֱזֶה
פָנֶיךָ אֶשְׂבְּעָה בְהָקִיץ
תְּמוּנָתֶךָ.

penny to the poor is deemed worthy to behold the face of the Divine Presence. For it is stated [in Scripture], *Through charity (ṣdq) I shall behold Your face, and I shall be satisfied when I awake with Your likeness* PS. 17:15.

רַבִּי אֶלְעָזָר נָתַן פְּרוּטָה
לְעָנִי וְאַחַר־כָּךְ הִתְפַּלֵּל;
אָמַר: הַכָּתוּב אוֹמֵר: אֲנִי
בְּצֶדֶק אֶחֱזֶה פָנֶיךָ.

B. Rabbi Eleazar once gave a penny to a poor person, and afterward prayed. [Later, he explained his actions,] saying, It is written [in Scripture], *Through charity (ṣdq) I shall behold Your face* PS. 17:15.

From the Jerusalem Talmud:

Horayot 3

The Reward of Tzedakah

מַעֲשֶׂה בְּרַבִּי אֶלִיעֶזֶר וְרַבִּי
יְהוֹשֻׁעַ וְרַבִּי עֲקִיבָא שֶׁהָלְכוּ
לְחוֹלַת אַנְטוֹכְיָא עַל עֵסֶק
מִגְבַּת צְדָקָה לַחֲכָמִים. הָיָה
שָׁם אֶחָד, אַבָּא־יוּדָן, שֶׁהָיָה
עוֹשֶׂה מִצְוָה בְּעַיִן יָפָה וְיָרַד
מִנְּכָסָיו. כֵּיוָן שֶׁרָאָה
רַבּוֹתֵינוּ נִתְכַּרְכְּמוּ פָּנָיו
וְהָלַךְ לְבֵיתוֹ. אָמְרָה לוֹ
אִשְׁתּוֹ: מִפְּנֵי מָה פָּנֶיךָ
חוֹלָנִיּוֹת? אָמַר לָהּ:
רַבּוֹתֵינוּ כָּאן וְאֵינִי יוֹדֵעַ

A. Rabbis Eliezer, Joshua, and Akiba went to the region of Antioch to collect charity (ṣdqh) for [needy] sages. [They found] there a person [called] Abba Yudan who [in the past] had generously performed the duty [of giving], but [by now] had lost all his wealth. When he saw the rabbis, Abba Yudan went home with a dejected face. His wife said to him, "Why do you look so sickly?" Abba Yudan replied, "The rabbis have come [to collect charity] and I don't know what to do." His wife, who was even more righteous (ṣdqt) than he, said to [Abba Yudan], "We still own one field; go sell half of it, and give [the proceeds] to [the rabbis]." This he went and did. The rabbis prayed for him and said, "Abba Yudan, may the Lord supply your needs." Some days later, [Abba Yudan] went out to plough the half-field [which remained] in his [possession]. As he was ploughing, the earth opened up, and [as a result] his cow slipped and broke [its hoof]. He bent down to help [his cow] up, and the Holy One, the Blessed, opened [Abba Yudan's] eyes, and revealed to him a treasure [beneath the cow]. Then [Abba Yudan] said, "[Surely] to my benefit has my cow broken its hoof."

B. When the rabbis returned to Antioch, they inquired about [the welfare of Abba Yudan]. They asked, "What is Abba Yudan doing [these days]?" The reply [they received] was, "Who sees Abba Yudan [these days]? For he is [so rich that he is surrounded by] slaves. He is Abba Yudan [possessor] of sheep; Abba Yudan [possessor] of asses; Abba Yudan [possessor] of camels; Abba Yudan [possessor] of

מָה אֶעֱשֶׂה. אִשְׁתּוֹ שֶׁהָיְתָה
צַדֶּקֶת מִמֶּנּוּ אָמְרָה לוֹ: לֹא
נִשְׁתַּיְּרָה לָנוּ אֶלָּא שָׂדֶה
אַחַת בִּלְבָד, לֵךְ מְכוֹר
חֶצְיָהּ וְתֵן לָהֶם. הָלַךְ
וְעָשָׂה כֵן. נִתְפַּלְּלוּ עָלָיו
רַבּוֹתֵינוּ וְאָמְרוּ לוֹ: אַבָּא־
יוּדָן, הַמָּקוֹם יְמַלֵּא
חֶסְרוֹנְךָ! לְאַחַר יָמִים יָצָא
לַחֲרֹשׁ בַּחֲצִי שָׂדֵהוּ. עִם
כְּשֶׁהוּא חוֹרֵשׁ נִבְקְעָה
הָאָרֶץ מִתַּחְתָּיו וְשָׁקְעָה
פָּרָתוֹ וְנִשְׁבְּרָה. יָרַד
לְהַעֲלוֹתָהּ, הֵאִיר הַקָּדוֹשׁ־
בָּרוּךְ־הוּא אֶת־עֵינָיו וּמָצָא
תַּחְתֶּיהָ מַטְמוֹן. אָמַר:
לְטוֹבָתִי נִשְׁבְּרָה רֶגֶל פָּרָתִי.

כְּשֶׁחָזְרוּ רַבּוֹתֵינוּ לְשָׁם
שָׁאֲלוּ עָלָיו וְאָמְרוּ: מָה
אַבָּא־יוּדָן עוֹשֶׂה? אָמְרוּ
לָהֶם: אַבָּא־יוּדָן — מִי
יָכוֹל לִרְאוֹת סֵבֶר־פָּנָיו?
הוּא אַבָּא־יוּדָן שֶׁל עֲבָדִים,
אַבָּא־יוּדָן שֶׁל עִזִּים, אַבָּא־
יוּדָן שֶׁל חֲמוֹרִים, אַבָּא־
יוּדָן שֶׁל גְּמַלִּים, אַבָּא־יוּדָן
שֶׁל שְׁוָרִים! כֵּיוָן שֶׁשָּׁמַע
אַבָּא־יוּדָן יָצָא לִקְרָאתָם.

אָמְרוּ לוֹ: מָה אַבָּא־יוּדָן
עוֹשֶׂה? אָמַר לָהֶם: עֶשְׂתָה
תְּפִלַּתְכֶם פֵּרוֹת וּפֵרֵי־
פֵרוֹת. אָמְרוּ לוֹ: חַיֶּיךָ, אַף־
עַל־פִּי שֶׁנָּתְנוּ אֲחֵרִים יוֹתֵר
מִמֶּךָ — אוֹתְךָ כָּתַבְנוּ רֹאשׁ
טִימוֹס. נְטָלוּהוּ וְהוֹשִׁיבוּהוּ
אֶצְלָם וְקָרְאוּ עָלָיו הַפָּסוּק
הַזֶּה: מַתָּן אָדָם יַרְחִיב לוֹ
וְלִפְנֵי גְדוֹלִים יַנְחֶנּוּ.

oxen!" When Abba Yudan heard [that the rabbis had returned], he came forth to greet them. [The rabbis] asked him, "What is Abba Yudan doing [these days]?" He replied, "Your prayer has borne fruit upon fruit." [The rabbis] said to him, "Although others gave more [charity] than you, we placed you at the top of our list." Then [the rabbis] seated Abba Yudan among them, and they recited for him the following verse [from Scripture], *A person's gift makes room for* [*that person*], *and brings* [*that person*] *before the great ones* PROV. 18:16.

From the Babylonian Talmud:

Kallah 51a

אָמְרוּ עָלָיו עַל רַבִּי טַרְפוֹן,
שֶׁהָיָה עָשִׁיר גָּדוֹל וְלֹא הָיָה
נוֹתֵן מַתָּנוֹת רַבּוֹת לָעֲנִיִּים.
פַּעַם אַחַת מְצָאוֹ רַבִּי
עֲקִיבָא. אָמַר לוֹ: רַבִּי,
רְצוֹנְךָ אֶקַּח לְךָ עִיר אַחַת
אוֹ שְׁתַּיִם? אָמַר לוֹ: הֵן.
מִיָּד עָמַד רַבִּי טַרְפוֹן וְנָתַן
לוֹ אַרְבָּעָה אֲלָפִים דִּינָרֵי
זָהָב. נְטָלָם רַבִּי עֲקִיבָא

They told the following story about Rabbi Tarfon. [Rabbi Tarfon was] very wealthy, but he did not give much charity to the poor. Once Rabbi Akiba met him, and said to him, "Master, would you like me to purchase for you one or two towns?" Rabbi Tarfon replied, "Yes," and promptly handed four thousand golden *dinars* to [Rabbi Akiba]. Rabbi Akiba took [the sum] and distributed it to some needy students. Some days later, Rabbi Tarfon met [Rabbi Akiba] and asked him, "Where are the towns which you have purchased for me?" [Rabbi Akiba] took him by the hand, brought him to the school, and summoned a pupil who was holding the book of Psalms. [The pupil] began reciting [verses from the book], and continued until he reached the following verse: *That person has distributed freely, that person has given to the poor, that person's righteousness (ṣdq) endures forever* PS. 112:9. [Then] Rabbi Akiba exclaimed, "This is the town which I have bought for you!" Rabbi Tarfon [immediately] embraced [Rabbi Akiba], and said to him, "My teacher, my superior—my teacher in wisdom, my superior in civil conduct," and [subsequently] gave [Rabbi Akiba] additional funds to distribute [to the needy].

וְחִלְּקָם לְתַלְמִידֵי־חֲכָמִים עֲנִיִּים. לְיָמִים מְצָאוֹ רַבִּי טַרְפוֹן, אָמַר לוֹ: הֵיכָן הָעֲיָרוֹת שֶׁלָּקַחְתָּ לִי? תְּפָסוֹ בְּיָדוֹ וְהוֹלִיכוֹ לְבֵית־הַמִּדְרָשׁ, וְהֵבִיא תִינוֹק וּבְיָדוֹ סֵפֶר תְּהִלִּים, וְהָיָה קוֹרֵא וְהוֹלֵךְ עַד שֶׁהִגִּיעַ לְפָסוּק זֶה: פִּזַּר נָתַן לָאֶבְיוֹנִים צִדְקָתוֹ עֹמֶדֶת לָעַד. אָמַר לוֹ: זוֹהִי הָעִיר שֶׁלָּקַחְתִּי לָךְ. עָמַד רַבִּי טַרְפוֹן וּנְשָׁקוֹ וְאָמַר לוֹ: רַבִּי, אַלוּפִי! רַבִּי בְּחָכְמָה וְאַלּוּפִי בְּדֶרֶךְ אֶרֶץ — וְהוֹסִיף לוֹ מָמוֹן לְבַזְּבֵּז.

From the Mishnah: Peah 1:1

אֵלּוּ דְבָרִים שֶׁאָדָם אוֹכֵל
פֵּרוֹתֵיהֶן בָּעוֹלָם הַזֶּה
וְהַקֶּרֶן קַיֶּמֶת לוֹ לָעוֹלָם
הַבָּא: כִּבּוּד אָב וָאֵם,
וּגְמִילוּת חֲסָדִים, וַהֲבָאַת
שָׁלוֹם בֵּין אָדָם לַחֲבֵרוֹ;
וְתַלְמוּד תּוֹרָה כְּנֶגֶד כֻּלָּם.

These are things, the return on which a person enjoys in this world, and the principal of which endures for the world-to-come: honoring one's father and mother, performing acts of loving-kindness, and bringing about peace between quarreling people; but the study of Torah is worth all of these put together.

Can Jewish Philanthropy Buy Jewish Survival?

From the Babylonian Talmud:

Baba Batra 9a

אָמַר רַב אַסִּי: שְׁקוּלָה
צְדָקָה כְּנֶגֶד כָּל־הַמִּצְוֹת.

Rabbi Assi said, Charity (ṣdqh) is as important as all the other commandments put together.